Joseph Lister
and Antisepsis

For Charlotte

My thanks are due to the Royal College of Surgeons of England for library facilities, and to my wife, Mary, and my secretary, Miss Jean Haseler, for their assistance in preparing and typing the manuscript.

A. J. Harding Rains

Joseph Lister (1827–1912)

Pioneers of Science and Discovery

Joseph Lister
and Antisepsis

AJ Harding Rains MS, FRCS

Professor of Surgery
Charing Cross Hospital Medical School,
University of London

Honorary Consultant Surgeon
Charing Cross Hospital

Member of Council
Royal College of Surgeons of England

Books in this Series

ISBN 0 85078 117 5
Copyright © 1977 Wayland Publishers Limited
First published in 1977 by Priory Press Limited,
49 Lansdowne Place, Hove, Sussex BN3 1HF
2nd impression 1978

Photoset, printed and bound
in Great Britain by
REDWOOD BURN LIMITED
Trowbridge & Esher

Contents

Illustrations

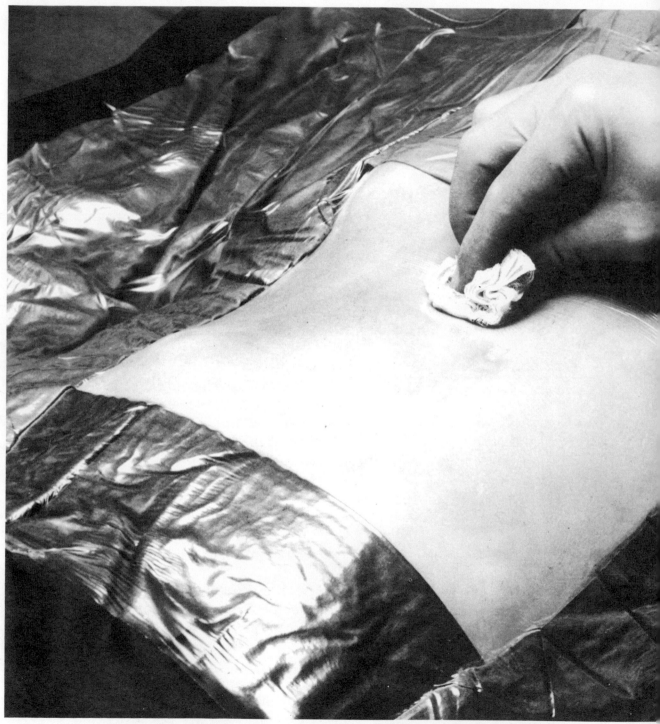

Above A modern barrier against infection. This sterile cling-film prevents bacteria from the skin infecting the open wound during an operation. It is a modern development of Lister's surgical principle of "antisepsis"—it literally works <u>against</u> sepsis.

An Introduction to Modern Surgery

Nobody likes the thought of being a patient in hospital and having an operation. Perhaps the fear is due to the need to have an anaesthetic. There is bound to be some discomfort or pain which will have to be lived through before the days of convalescence and that "I'm getting better every day" feeling.

Patients nowadays can be confident that operations are safe because they are in the hands of surgeons who are trained up to high standards of care and operating skill. But if they were able to talk to people in hospital a hundred years ago they would hear that surgery was far from safe, even in the hands of skilled and dedicated surgeons. Then, the chances of surviving an operation were only 50/50, and much less if an arm or leg had to be amputated. As soon as the skin was torn badly, for example by a broken bone, or cut into by a surgeon's scalpel, there was the risk that the flesh would rot and the body be consumed by blood poisoning. This was called sepsis. Surgeons would perform only those few operations which were absolutely necessary, and they would probably admit that recovery was a matter of chance and luck.

Why did this sepsis occur? What could be done to make surgery safe? In 1865 Joseph Lister, an English surgeon working in Glasgow, solved the puzzle. He was quick to see a meaning in the experiments of the French chemist, Louis Pasteur. Pasteur believed that "germs" or "microbes" in the air—which were too small to be seen—caused the fermentation of wine. Lister, supposing germs in the air were the unseen "living assassins" (bacteria) invading his patients, waged war against them—anti sepsis. He used carbolic acid as his first line of attack, as well as his defence. Immediately the fortunes of his patients changed, and he spent the next twelve years convincing other surgeons at home and abroad. His antiseptic methods made it possible for surgeons to introduce all kinds of new life-saving and life-improving operations.

"The Father of Modern Surgery" is the title by which Lister is to be remembered. All the complicated and remarkable operations of today, including transplant and spare-part surgery, depend ultimately upon the use of antiseptic chemicals, heat, atomic irradiation and other barriers to bacterial contamination. Lister's message is clear, the success of any operation depends primarily upon an unrelenting battle against sepsis, i.e. anti sepsis. Any slackness, or slip-up in technique, and the patient is immediately in peril.

Top right   Joseph Lister's mother and father, Isabella Lister and Joseph Jackson Lister. The picture of Isabella was drawn by her husband.

Bottom right   Upton House in West Ham, London, where Joseph Lister was born on the 5th April, 1827. After a drawing by Mary Lister (Joseph's sister).

1 *The Life of Joseph Lister*

It is often thought that Lister was a Scotsman. He was in fact a Londoner, though his family came from Yorkshire farming stock. In 1720 his great grandfather came to London to work as a tobacconist, leaving his home at Bingley, a town on the Yorkshire moors near Haworth, the home of the Brontë family. Joseph's grandfather was an apprenticed watchmaker but he became a wine merchant in the City of London and did well. Joseph's father, Joseph Jackson Lister, became more than a successful wine merchant, for his special hobby was the microscope. He invented a lens which allowed him to see minute objects more clearly than ever before, free from being seen in light which was often distorted with the colours of the rainbow. For this scientific work on what are called achromatic lenses he was elected a Fellow of the Royal Society (FRS). It has been said that he achieved this fame from a bubble. This is because, when he was a child, he suffered from poor eyesight and found that by looking through a bubble of air in a glass window-pane he could see objects in the garden more clearly. He married a school-mistress, Isabella Harris, who came from a Cumberland family, and they had three children, Arthur, Joseph and Mary.

Joseph Lister was born on the 5th April, 1827, at Upton House, West Ham, London. It was a large mansion, surrounded by a big garden and beyond was open countryside providing good opportunities for nature study. At that time the railway and the housing development that sprawled with it were not yet built.

The Lister family were Quakers and Joseph was raised in an atmosphere of simplicity and quiet be-

haviour. In the spoken or written word he would address another as "thee" or "thou". He went to Quaker schools at Hitchin, Hertfordshire, and Tottenham (The Grove School) between 1835 and 1844. He excelled in learning German and French and in studying botany.

Lister had already decided to become a doctor. He was enrolled as a student of University College to study for the matriculation examination and then the Bachelor of Arts (BA) degree of the University of London. He could not be taught in King's College because at that time only members of the Church of England could be admitted there. The non-conformists and free thinkers had to look elsewhere for higher educational opportunities. Thirty-three years later, however, Lister returned to London to become Professor of Surgery at King's College Hospital.

In October, 1846, while Joseph was reading for his BA, the first operation in Britain to be carried out under an ether general anaesthetic was performed by Mr Robert Liston at University College Hospital. Possibly young Joseph may have been present. Little could he have known then that, in spite of this new boon to humanity, modern surgery could not develop

Mar 15 Yesterday Mr Erichsen at his visit passed a silver catheter, no
urine flowed from it but it went in with a jerk, & was in tight: it
was left in about an hour. About 9 o'clock last-night he had
"the cold shivers" very badly, lasting about half an hour, as if
his flesh was creeping from his bones: a hot bottle to his feet
gave him some relief. about an hour after his bowels were
a good deal affected; he went three times to stool & had much
tenesmus: went last to stool about 12 o'clock. He is now better
(10 A.M.) but has had no medicine: some brandy early in the
morning did him good. Pulse 84 full but compressible, tongue
clean: mouth very dry last night now moist.   He says
his bowels are wont to be a good deal affected by passage
of the catheter, but he never had rigors before: but has had
spasms (of the neck of the bladder or urethral muscles apparently)
his bowels being at the same time as much affected as by
a dose of physic. The membranous urethra (the prostatic part
apparently) feels a little sore this morning.

" 16 Yesterday afternoon about 3 o'clock another shivering fit-
was coming on, but averted by brandy & water.

" 18 Having a cough & tightness of the chest he was ordered

                    R.   Mist. Acaciæ c̄ Vino Ipecac. ℥j ter diebus
This medicine was serviceable to him.

" 20 The left side of the scrotum is now almost as much
as the right, & both nearly of the natural size: the right
side is nearly in the normal condition: one small brawny
part still existing at the lowest part of the scrotum. The
left side is more extensively brawny at the lower part-; but
the upper part- is quite soft & in the natural condition.
Cough better: Bowels still somewhat relaxed. He is
to take some of the penetrate of iron mixture out with
him. He is discharged today, being made an outpatient
to come when he gets a little stronger, to have the condition
of the urethra ascertained; The poultice has been
continued up to this time & he is to continue its application.

                              Joseph Lister Dresser.

until he, Joseph Lister, was to release it from the chains of hospital infection which had bound it for centuries.

In 1848, before he became a medical student in the hospital, he was struck down by another enemy of mankind, smallpox. One can only suppose he had not been given the benefit of Dr Jenner's discovery of vaccination, made in 1796. Foolishly he tried to return to his studies too soon and was overtaken by what is now called a nervous breakdown. A proper period of recovery—convalescence—in Ireland was ordered and by the end of the year he began two years of hospital work. He enjoyed the activities of the student societies and, although he was a Quaker, those occasional light-hearted foolish pranks and brushes with authority in the medical school and hospital which were part of a medical student's life.

He was never slack in his work. Besides attending all the classes and the work in the hospital wards he found time to carry out some original research on the eye and the skin under the supervision of two of his teachers (Chapter 4). He was able to publish his results in a science journal soon after becoming a doctor.

It is not surprising that such hard work and enthusiasm was rewarded by very high marks and two university gold medals when he took the degree of Bachelor of Medicine and Surgery (MB, BS London) in 1850. Afterwards he had no difficulty in passing the difficult Fellowship examination of the Royal College of Surgeons of England (FRCS) in 1852, and in the training for this he must have been grateful to his surgical master and chief Mr (later Sir) John Ericksen.

It was customary to encourage young surgeons and doctors to visit continental medical centres as part of their training and further education. However, Professor Sharpey, the physiologist who helped Lister with his early research, advised him to first

Left Professor James Syme. Lister became Syme's house surgeon in Edinburgh.

Below Professor Syme's daughter Agnes. She and Joseph Lister were married on the 23rd April, 1856.

spend a month in Edinburgh with a brilliant surgeon friend of his, Professor James Syme. Instead of staying for a month in 1853, Lister stayed in Scotland for the next twenty-four years!

The introductory visit resulted in a chance of becoming Syme's house surgeon and assistant and, therefore, of getting more experience in caring for patients and teaching students. And there was another attraction in Edinburgh, Agnes, the Professor's daughter, and she was attracted to Joseph.

He was a handsome, athletic-looking young man, about 5 feet 10 inches in height, with dark curly hair and side whiskers, and clear, steady grey eyes. He had a serene and kindly face which, we are told, hardly ever broke into a smile. A slight stutter in his speech over certain consonants did not spoil his ability as a good speaker and lecturer.

Joseph and Agnes were married in Syme's house (Millbank, Morningside, Edinburgh) on the 23rd April, 1856, and since Joseph could not remain a Quaker if he married out of the Society of Friends he had to resign from that Society. He joined his wife as a member of the Episcopalian Church. They spent their honeymoon in the Lake District and in Italy, and they returned to live in 11 Rutland Street.

Agnes always took a great interest in her husband's work and she helped him with his research experiments and in writing up his notes. Although childless, their happy and loving relationship continued for thirty-eight years. Agnes died of pneumonia while they were visiting Italy, the country of their honeymoon, in 1893.

Joseph was promoted to Assistant Surgeon and Lecturer in Surgery in 1856. He had gained the Diploma of FRCS Edinburgh in 1855 and by 1857 was fully competent to take charge of a ward while his seniors were on holiday. He was now quite capable of performing the operations of those days, restricted as they were by hospital infection. His popularity with

his students earned him the nickname of "The Chief", a name which stuck to him for the rest of his career.

It was unusual for students to see a surgeon who used a microscope, for Joseph was continuing with his researches. By the time he was thirty-three years old his work on the early stages of inflammation was judged to be of sufficient merit for him to be elected a Fellow of the Royal Society (1860). No wonder that a young surgeon of such promise should be appointed Regius Professor of Surgery in Glasgow in 1860. He and Agnes moved to 17 Woodside Place where he prepared for the customary ordeal of delivering, in Latin, his first address (on the teaching of surgery) to the University.

In Glasgow he was given a great deal of support by the students when he found that he needed hospital beds in which to treat patients. It was not until November, 1861, that he performed an operation there. But from then on he began to plan new oper-

Above The surgical hospital of the Old Royal Infirmary, Edinburgh, in which Professor James Syme and Lister taught and worked.

16

ations, new techniques, and to improve anaesthetics and to reduce the shock of operations. He was full of ideas.

1864 was not a good year because he was disappointed in his attempt to return to Edinburgh as a Professor. Also his mother died, and in his own earnest and loving way he began to write to his father every week.

1865, on the other hand, was the year of his great discovery. Like every other surgeon, Lister was distressed by infection, the dreaded complication of almost every operation. Infection got out of hand and turned to a kind of rotting (putrefaction) of the skin and flesh which finally destroyed the patient by blood poisoning. Progress in surgery was really quite impossible because of this degree of infection, which is also known as sepsis.

Lister's problem was even worse because his accident ward was built beside a burial pit. Fortunately, his long interest in research had prepared his mind to interpret some news given him by a colleague. A French chemist, Louis Pasteur, had shown that fermentation must be caused by yet unseen microbes (bacteria) in the air. Lister immediately thought that the sepsis that occurred in his patients might be due to microbes and he tried out the effect of a dressing containing a crude type of carbolic acid which had been found effective in treating sewage in Carlisle. The first tests in 1865 were encouraging and by March and April 1867 he was able to publish a collection of successful cases in the medical journal *The Lancet*. From that moment surgery was released from the shackles which had prevented its development, and patients who would have died, now lived. The dawn of modern surgery had appeared.

By now Lister was forty and for the next twenty-six years he devoted himself to perfecting antiseptic techniques using carbolic acid in a spray form and as a solution during all operations. When he appreciated

Below Joseph Lister. The photograph was taken at about the time his articles on the antiseptic principle appeared in *The Lancet*. He was then aged 40.

that bacteria and, therefore, infection could be spread by water, he used an antiseptic at every stage of an operation. His technique was truly antiseptic (against sepsis) and he, therefore, prepared others to develop the use of heat and other methods to exclude bacteria from open wounds in operating theatres. He made surgical materials safe to use and really founded the idea of modern spare-part surgery.

Lister endured a great deal of opposition and apathy to his new technique. He overcame this by his writings, his lectures, his demonstrations and the encouraging news of the turn of the tide in his favour in countries like Denmark and Germany. By 1879 the anti septic principle was accepted.

Left Charlotte Square, Edinburgh. No. 9 is the second house from the left. Joseph and Agnes lived here during the time he was Professor of Clinical Surgery at the Royal Infirmary.

Below In later years, when he was a celebrated man, Lister travelled a great deal. This snapshot, taken by Lord Polwarth, shows Lister on board *SS Parisian*. Lister, aged 70, was on his way out to the 1897 meeting of the British Medical Association in Montreal, Canada.

During those years between 1867 and 1879 he was able to return to Edinburgh as the Professor after Professor Syme had retired. He and Agnes lived at 9 Charlotte Square. Besides defending and extending his antiseptic technique he continued with his nature study. This included finding out why cow's milk goes sour, and calling the bacteria which does this, *Bacterium Lactis*. He was indeed a pioneer bacteriologist. He studied the moulds which sometimes grow on food and he made drawings of Penicillium. But the discovery of the drug derived from this mould—penicillin—had to await the work of Alexander Fleming in 1929.

Although he loved Edinburgh and the chance and the happiness, through Agnes, that it had given him, he knew that the final victory for his great work on antisepsis would depend upon its acceptance in his native London. Because of this he became Professor of Surgery in King's College Hospital in 1877, living near Regent's Park at 12 Park Crescent, at the end of Portland Place. At first his conversion of the London surgeons to antisepsis was heavy going but by 1879 he succeeded.

In his last fifteen years of active surgery Lister was in great demand as a lecturer in Britain and overseas. He was a great medical ambassador, and his service to mankind was acclaimed everywhere and honours and awards were showered upon him. He was a member of Council and Vice-President of the Royal College of Surgeons of England, the President of the British Association for the Advancement of Science, and President of the Royal Society.

In 1871 he operated upon Queen Victoria. He became Sir Joseph in 1883 and Lord Lister in 1897 (the first medical Peer). He was one of the first members of the Order of Merit (OM), and also a Privy Councillor (PC). He received the freedoms of the cities of Edinburgh, London and Glasgow. In London an Institute of Preventive Medicine, based on the idea of the Pasteur Institute in France, to provide vaccines to prevent and cure infective diseases, was named after him.

In 1903 he became ill and was badly troubled by his failing sight, painful joints and general weakness. He moved to Walmer in Kent in 1908 and died, as his wife had done, of pneumonia on the 10th February, 1912, aged eighty-five. The general desire for burial in Westminster Abbey was set aside by his own wish and, after a great funeral service in the Abbey, he was buried beside his dear wife in Hampstead cemetery.

Top right   Queen Victoria

Bottom right   Edward VII

Left   Lister's tombstone
in Hampstead cemetary.

20

2 Lister's World

During Joseph Lister's lifetime five monarchs were to sit on the throne of Great Britain: George IV, William IV, Queen Victoria, Edward VII and George V. Our record of Joseph's life and achievements identifies him with three of these: namely, William IV, Queen Victoria and Edward VII.

As a small boy of only eight years he actually wrote to King William asking if he could visit him to see him on his throne, with his crown on his head and his sceptre in his hand.

It was many years later, in 1871, that Lister found himself before majesty when he was called to perform an operation on Queen Victoria, as by this time he was her surgeon in Scotland. The Queen was suffering from an abscess in her armpit. An abscess contains pus and bacteria and needs to be opened with a knife otherwise the patient will become seriously ill with blood poisoning (septicaemia) from the bacteria causing the infection. Her Majesty bore the operation very well (Chapter 7), remarking that it was "A most disagreeable duty most agreeably performed".

In 1902 another royal abscess required the presence of Lister. Immediately before his coronation King Edward VII became seriously ill from acute appendicitis which had formed an abscess. Lister was surgeon to the King. A momentous decision had to be made to postpone the coronation ceremony and instead to operate on the abscess. Sir Frederick Treves performed the operation. Later, when Lister was honoured by being made a Privy Councillor, King Edward said, "Lord Lister, I know well that if it had not been for you and your work I would not have been here today."

Troubles sometimes come in threes, so it is interesting that some fourteen years after Lister's death, King George V had an abscess in his chest following pneumonia. Here again Listerian methods would have to be followed and the abscess properly drained by inserting a drainage tube (Chapter 7).

Both Queen Victoria and King Edward VII sought the advice of Lister on other matters. For example, Queen Victoria was shocked at the use of animals for experiments and Lister received a letter asking him to condemn such experiments. In a long reply Lister said that he could not do this since in the beginning his research had been dependent on frogs and bats, and then the only way he could find out how really successful his antiseptic techniques were was to use a mammal, such as a horse or a calf. He was worried lest the chance of further discoveries in science would be stopped by complete abolition of the use of animals for this work. In the end a compromise was reached in the Cruelty to Animals Act of 1876, and since then any work using an animal cannot be done without a licence in a registered animal house which is regularly inspected. In Britain no-one can use animals just to practise ordinary operations.

King Edward was, however, interested in the development of health services for the nation, particularly hospitals, and many are named after him as well as the Fund which helps to try out new ideas in the hospital care of patients.

The year of 1848 is worthy of recall in the light of the events which were taking place in the world. Lister was about to become a medical student in University College Hospital, but he caught smallpox and this was followed by a nervous breakdown which may have been caused by the effects of smallpox and also by world events.

It must be remembered that Joseph was a Quaker and took life and work very seriously. He may well

Above Newcastle-upon-Tyne. Railways and the Industrial Revolution changed the face of Britain in the mid-19th century.

have felt great natural concern for the state of England in those days. Other Quakers, related or near friends of the family like Elizabeth Fry, were much concerned with the state of the poor and those in prison. The wars against France ending with the defeat of Napoleon had cost the country dearly; it was greatly in debt. Some kind of social security had to be provided for the wounded and the families of those who had died in those wars. The industrial revolution had started off the present mechanical age and the growth of industrial towns and railways. The needs of the farmers and the farm labourers had to be balanced against the demands to relieve the miseries of the people in the towns. 1848 is associated with, and the end of, fifteen previous years of Corn Laws, the Reform Bill, trouble in Ireland, the Tolpuddle Martyrs, deportation to Australia and Canada for the poor and unemployed, strikes, a people's charter (Chartism), the Communist Manifesto of Karl Marx and Friedrich Engels, and many uprisings in Europe.

Small wonder then that a sensitive and serious young Quaker, dedicated to being a surgeon to help humanity, should feel unstable. Students, though idealists and rightly so, like a harbour of stability at their backs. Lister was advised to recuperate in Ireland and during this holiday the letter which his father wrote to him illustrates not only the Quaker manner of speaking but also the relationship between father and son on the serious matters of life:

". . . it is indeed a mistake . . . to believe thyself required to bear burthens on account of the states of others. . . . And believe us, my tenderly beloved son, that thy proper part now is to cherish a pious cheerful spirit, open to see and to enjoy the bounties and the beauties spread around us . . . not to give way to turning thy thoughts upon thyself nor even at present to dwell long on serious things."

It might have been on the eve of his entry to the hospital as what was called a "dresser" that Lister somehow felt that he was embarking on a great mission to do something for suffering humanity. In the crowded wards of a busy hospital, dressing the wounds which were probably already septic and foul-smelling, he must have noticed how poorly nourished most of the ordinary working people and their families were, and that the wounds of the most undernourished seemed to lack vitality and never healed properly.

It was not known then that infections spread most quickly where there is overcrowding and undernourishment. And, in addition to the infection of wounds, tuberculosis of the lungs or bones and joints spreads quickly because of these factors. Even today in Africa and Asia, where there is plenty of sunshine and fresh air but where undernourishment prevails, disease strikes hard.

In Lister's day it was Florence Nightingale who recognized that the nourishment of a patient, particularly the wounded soldier, was a most important element of care. Miss Nightingale's message to us, and her views on proper hospital planning and overcrowding, took a long time to be accepted and they—like Lister's message—were, and still are, always in danger of being forgotten. No wonder that Joseph Lister, the young medical student, was shaken into puzzling why the dreadful scenes of infection could not be changed.

While he knew of social upheavals, Lister also lived at a time when there were many famous men and women in literature, art and science. Examples of almost exact contemporaries include, respectively, Tolstoy, Jules Verne, Lewis Carroll, Thomas Hardy and George Eliot; Manet, Millais and Pissaro; Pasteur and Nobel. Like other contemporaries, Miss Florence Nightingale who revolutionised nursing care, and his senior in surgery, Sir James Simpson

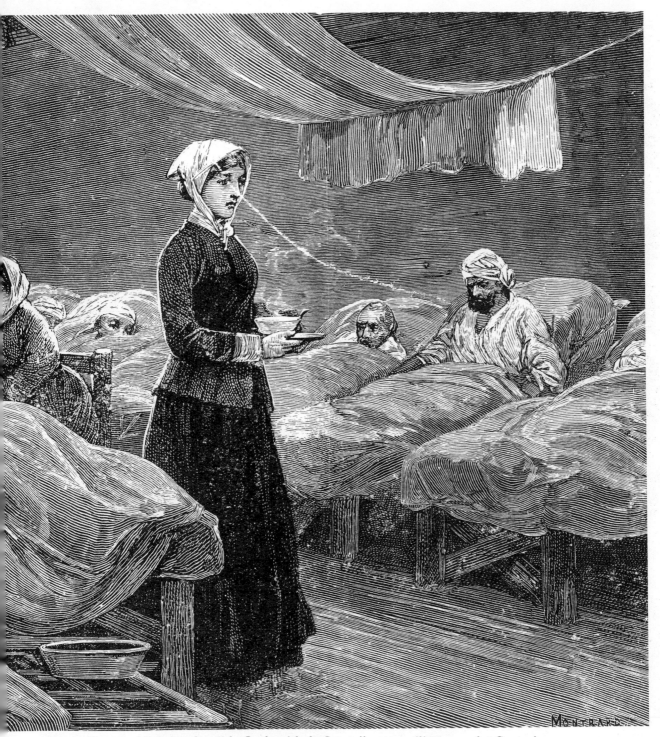

Above Florence Nightingale—"the Lady with the Lamp"—on a military ward at Scutari during the Crimean War. She was one of the first to recognize that overcrowding in hospitals increased the risk of infection.

who introduced chloroform as an anaesthetic, he fitted well into this scene and provided British medicine with world-wide fame.

As a Quaker who knew his Bible and the story of Adam and Eve, he must have had an opinion about the work of Charles Darwin on evolution (1859), and the support of Darwin by the famous physiologist Professor Huxley. And, too, about the dispute these two had with the Church, particularly with Bishop Wilberforce over what appeared to be a challenge to the first chapter of Genesis. If he did, we do not know. Darwin himself was very interested in Lister's work and wrote in 1878 to suggest an alternative antiseptic to carbolic acid, namely, benzoic acid, a chemical which was used for years as a preservative to prevent food (e.g. sausages) from going bad.

Another distinguished contemporary scientist was William Thompson, Professor of Physics at Glasgow University. Lister, even on the brink of his own discovery, was delighted that Thompson's work on the Atlantic cable, laid by the pride of Britain, the *SS Great Eastern*, was successful. Professor Thompson became Lord Kelvin. Thirty-two years later Kelvin was to write to congratulate Lister on becoming Lord Lister.

The year of Lister's first attempts to conquer hospital infections by carbolic acid, 1865, coincided with the death of Dr. Ignaz Semmelweis. He was the Hungarian doctor who, quite unknown to Lister, had discovered that hospital infection can be spread by unwashed hands. Other events of that year, though marked by the end of the American Civil War and overshadowed by the assassination of Abraham Lincoln, included the experiments on heredity by Mendel. In London General Booth founded the Salvation Army.

Lister, like General Booth and Abraham Lincoln, was sensitive to human needs. He was always saddened by the thought that his discovery came too late to help save the lives of those wounded in the Crimean War and the American Civil War. He grieved especially over the failure of the surgical world to recognize his discovery and to use his antiseptic technique to treat the large numbers of wounded in the Franco-Prussian War of 1870. The wounded in later wars in Egypt and in South Africa were much more fortunate because Listerism, as antisepsis was then called, had been accepted everywhere.

Right A scene of carnage from the Battle of St Quentin, fought during the Franco-Prussian War of 1870. The lives of many of the wounded might have been saved, if army surgeons had adopted Lister's antiseptic techniques.

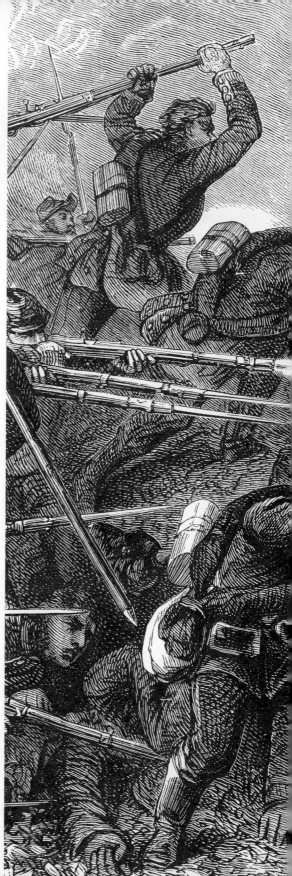

Below A contemporary drawing showing the assassination of Abraham Lincoln, President of the United States, in 1865. In the same year, Lister first experimented with carbolic acid as an antiseptic.

3 Science through Nature Study

"My dear cousin Rachel I hope thou will accept this little drawing in one of the leaves of the books, that thee gave me. . . ."

This note, with the drawing of a frog and a lizard made when he was eight, is a good example of Lister's early interest in nature study. In the same year he wrote to his sister, Mary, and enclosed a painting of a blue and yellow crocus. Previously between 1831 and

Below The letter from Lister, aged 8, to his cousin Rachel.

1834 he had drawn quite good pictures of horses, birds and other animals. Of course he was lucky to have grown up in West Ham while it was still countryside, and it was possible to walk into London along a path beside the Thames. Both Mary and Rachel were good at botany while his brother, Arthur, a well-known ornithologist (bird watcher) was also world famous for his work on minute fungi. Arthur's daughter, Gulielma, followed the fame of her father, while his son, another Joseph, studied butterflies and marine biology in which he became an expert, particularly in the tiny chalk animals called *foramenifera*.

So the family interest in nature study was strong. Young Lister in his schooldays wrote one essay on bones (osteology) and another on the likeness between a man and a monkey. He dissected fish and when he was fourteen he put together the skeleton of a frog. In a letter to his father he writes:

"It looks just as if it was going to take a leap, and I stole one of Mary's pieces of wood . . . to stick it down upon and put it on the top of the cabinet with a small bell glass over it. . . . Do not tell Mary about the piece of wood."

As a student, Lister was greatly encouraged by a botanist, Professor Lindley, who taught him how to press flowers and sort them into families and races. Fifty years previously a Swedish doctor, Linnaeus, had discovered this was possible. Lister's interest in botany continued throughout his lifetime and he enjoyed identifying and collecting specimens of plant life, especially alpine plants, during frequent holidays in the highlands of Scotland and the mountains of Central Europe.

On the 20th August, 1851, another milestone in nature study is represented in a letter to his father from Shanklin, Isle of Wight, a holiday place used years before by the doctor-poet, John Keats. We can imagine Joseph has just returned from discovering the pools in the "Horseledges", which are exposed at low tide below the cliffs and to the west of Shanklin Chine. The sea there makes sucking and blowing noises through the holes in the flat rocks. He has been looking at specimens with the microscope which he always carried with him:

"I succeeded pretty well with the shrimps . . . looking at them with the 2/3 glass in the trough I saw the peristaltic action of the intestinal canal, the heart beating very rapidly . . . the aorta pulsating . . . the rapid arterial currents . . . but more interesting still to me the blood slowly returning over the surface of the limbs and over the back to the heart, its motion

Above An extract from the young Lister's essay on osteology, written about 1840, while he was still at school.

Above The path down to the beach at Shanklin Chine, Isle of Wight. It was on a visit to Shanklin in 1851—aged 24—that Lister was able to study the blood circulation of shrimps with the aid of his microscope.

Left Lister, aged 13. The silhouette was done by his father.

being indicated by the very distinct blood corpuscles. I even saw, as I believe, a valve in the middle of the upper part of the heart alternately open and close at each pulse. . . . I had a glorious bathe today and swam 52 yards in 2 minutes."

This incident reveals an early scientific interest in the circulation of the blood in the tiny blood vessels (capillaries) of animals and men. It was perhaps the starting point of his experiments on inflammation (Chapter 5) which helped him in his quest to solve the problem of hospital infection.

Fourteen years later when he made the breakthrough and became famous he embarked on a new kind of nature study, the study of minute living things as seen down the microscope—what is nowadays

34

Louis Pasteur.

Above A swan-necked flask used by Lister. For his later experiments with milk he used wineglasses (*below*). The wineglass A and its glass cap B were sterilized by heating. But the piece of plate glass D, and the bell glass C were not. Although air could get through, dust and bacteria could not, so the milk in the glass did not turn sour.

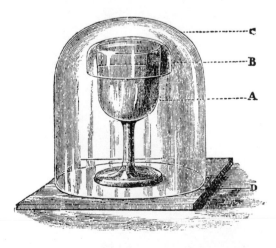

called microbiology. A Dutchman, Antony van Leeuwenhoek, had invented the microscope in 1675 and through it he saw tiny animals which he called animiculae. The trouble was that no-one knew what these tiny living creatures did in the world of nature. In the world of medicine the definite connection between such a plant/animal (a yeast or a bacterium) and a particular disease was not confirmed until the work of the German, Dr. Robert Koch (1843–1910). Dr. Koch was to microbiology as Dr. Linnaeus was to botany. Both sorted things out.

Lister with his microscope could at least see yeasts, and as he liked to observe tiny living creatures he made what he called his glass garden—a small glass chamber with a glass cover—so he could keep the contents alive and observe them through the microscope. Thus he would see yeasts growing and sprouting buds and changing in form over a period of hours, days or even weeks if need be.

Lister was one of the first people to understand the demonstration by Louis Pasteur that there must be germs in the air which cause the fermentation of wine. It was not due to "spontaneous generation" or caused by oxygen in the air. Perhaps the fact that Lister's father was a wine merchant had something to do with this interest.

Lister, while he was Professor of Surgery in Edinburgh and in London and spreading the good news about antisepsis, performed experiments with wine and milk. He found, like Pasteur, that if these fluids were heated in a glass flask and the neck of the flask was bent over so that air but not dirt could re-enter the flask, no fermentation or putrefaction would take place. For the hundreds of experiments he performed he chose wineglasses, for he was able to heat these and then syphon in heated milk and cover them with a glass cover which had also been heated. He found that heated milk would not go sour. At the same time he found that, provided many strict antiseptic precautions were taken, it was indeed possible to keep milk from a cow and stop it going sour. And so these experiments led him to think that there was a particular germ (bacterium) which caused the souring of milk. At first he got mixed up with other bacteria and moulds and Pasteur helped him in this by correspondence. Eventually he was able to produce a pure culture of a bacterium he called *Bacterium Lactis*, a remarkable achievement in those days. Since then similar germs have been recognised as starting off the changes in milk necessary to make cheeses and yoghurt.

There was yet another exciting event in his life of nature study. He found a strange mould growing on food, such as meat paste, and he made a careful drawing. It was *Penicillium*, a type of mould which Alexander Fleming, some sixty years later, was to find capable of destroying bacteria which cause disease. We might call *Penicillium* one of nature's living antiseptics, though we, in fact, call it an antibiotic. We are left wondering if Lister, being the brilliant observer of nature he was, could in time have made the antibiotic discovery himself.

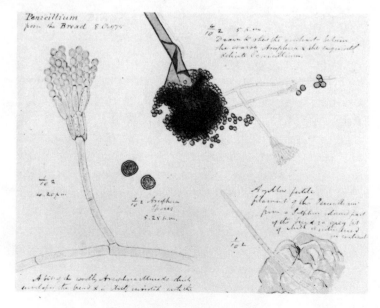

Left Lister's drawing of the Penicillium mould, dated the 8th October, 1875.

36

4 Research as a Student

It is often said that Lister's chief weapon in his fight against wound infection was the microscope. We might add that he started with an advantage. It was a happy chance that his father was a leading microscopist of the country, and amongst his relatives were the Beck family who actually built these new tools of biological research.

But even with the best microscope Lister had to learn to ask "What am I looking at?" and "What am I looking for?", and further "Who will teach me?" and "What line might yield to further study?".

It was again a happy chance. The medical course began with the teaching of the anatomy (structure) and the physiology (function) of the human body. Lister found himself in the hands of good teachers, in particular, Professor Sharpey the physiologist and Professor Wharton Jones who was one of the first eye specialists.

History has left few traces of Wharton Jones, but to have once been called "one of the greatest Englishmen who ever lived" must mean something. It is certain that he did much to stimulate two of our great nineteenth century medical scientists, Joseph Lister and Professor Thomas Huxley, and both acknowledged their debt to him. It would seem that he knew how to share his ideas fully with good students and to help them to ask questions and to undertake projects of their own. It was a good form of education which was to become known as the heuristic method, one which favours future discoveries and inventions. The great British aeronautical engineer of this century, Sir Barnes Wallis, is another product of this method.

So while Lister was a medical student he began projects and wrote scientific papers which were fin-

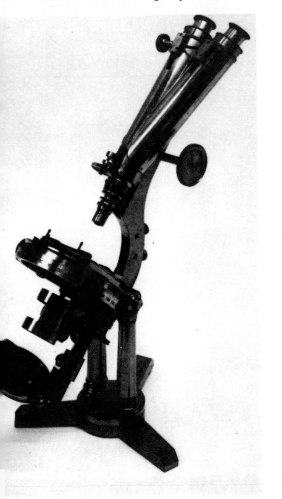

Below This microscope was made to Lister's own design by his cousins Richard and Joseph Beck.

ished and published soon after he became a doctor and surgeon in training. Amongst the subjects were his observations on the muscular tissue of the iris and on the muscular fibres of the skin.

A German, Professor Kolliker, who afterwards became a life-long friend of Lister, was the first to find out that tiny cells of muscle can be found in various parts of the body. This kind of muscle is called smooth muscle. Unlike the muscles (striped muscle) which move the face, arms and legs under the control of our voluntary will, smooth muscles contract and relax in an involuntary way beyond conscious will-power. So they are called involuntary muscles. The Professor had discovered these muscles in the coloured part of the eye, the iris. He deduced that it is these muscles that alter the aperture of the iris (the pupil) according to the amount of light shining into the eye and the amount of focussing required for the clear view of an object, just like the adjustment required for a camera.

Wharton Jones had found the same as Professor Kolliker but he asked Lister to study this in greater depth and to dissect a human eye that he, as an eye surgeon, had removed. Lister studied the human iris and then the iris in animals and found that there are two layers of iris muscle. There is one which contracts the pupil when facing a bright light and one which enlarges it (dilates it) in the dark. One can imagine the beautiful drawings Lister made of these muscles.

The other study extended Professor Kolliker's work on the same kind of muscle fibres which make the hair stand on end (with "goose pimples") when one is exposed to cold or is frightened. It is a reaction best seen when a cat meets a strange dog. Lister improved on these observations and, besides making the first detailed drawings of these muscle fibres, found that they could be best demonstrated in the skin of the scalp.

A third project was carried out while Lister was a house surgeon. Previously it was imagined that particles of food might pass directly through the wall of the intestine into the tiny channels (called lacteals) that run from the intestines. From there it was thought that they would collect in one final duct (called the thoracic duct) leading through the chest into the neck, to empty into the vein in the neck (the jugular vein) and so into the blood. So Lister mixed a little indian ink with some bread and milk, and fed this to mice and then looked at these lacteals with his microscope. He was able to settle that no solid particle of food as such passed into the blood.

One may well ask—"How was it that a medical student and doctor with all the ordinary work of learning and caring for patients could have enough energy and time to spare for research and be able to collect two university gold medals during the medical course?" Well, it was done by sheer hard and dedicated work at all hours of the day and night.

Below Lister's interest in research through the use of the microscope continued right through his working life. The sketch below—drawn in 1873— shows "bone from the interior of a loose cartilage".

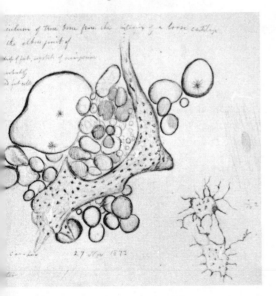

5 *The Glorious Nights*

By now we can picture a young surgeon in training who, on moving to Edinburgh to learn more practical surgery under Professor Syme, continues with his skill in research. He is already interested in tiny smooth muscle cells which respond involuntarily outside our conscious control. He has seen them in the eye and in the skin. Now he begins to study their presence and action in the blood vessels. He observes how the red corpuscles of the blood move through the tiny blood vessels called capillaries. As already mentioned in Chapter 3, the holiday in Shanklin may have started something.

Above "The Chief" and his associates in the summer of 1854, at the Old Royal Infirmary, Edinburgh. Standing: John Kirk, George Hogarth Pringle, Patrick Heron Watson. Seated: John Beddoe, Joseph Lister, David Christison, Alexander Struthers. All of these young doctors, except Alexander Struthers who died at Scutari, 1855, went on to have long and distinguished careers.

It was during the years 1855–58 that he spent the "glorious nights" of making observations on the web of the frog, a cold-blooded animal, or the wing of the bat, a warm-blooded animal. He had to do this after a full day's work in the operating theatre, the hospital wards and the lecture theatres of the medical school. He describes his feelings at the beginning of this period to his father:

"I am now really doing work: I have long wished to see the process of inflammation in the frog's foot, and, as I think I once told thee, felt that the early stages of the process had not been traced as they might be, so as to see the transition from a state of healthy increased redness to inflammation . . . having got a frog from Duddington Lock . . . I proceeded last evening to the investigation. Mr. Sparshott . . . kindly assisted me, and a most glorious night I had of it. . . ."

Using the microscope he observed the circulation of the red blood corpuscles flowing from the small arteries through the capillaries into the veins. He noted that the size of a capillary was just large enough to allow one corpuscle through at a time. Then he tried the effect of hot water on the web, and gradually increased the temperature and the number of times he applied this kind of heat. At first the capillaries would become larger (dilate) allowing corpuscles to pass three abreast and then would contract to normal size. With increasing injury there was no return to normal and the capillaries became stuffed with corpuscles and they became sticky and the blood clotted (coagulated).

Lister repeated this kind of experiment many times and always produced the same effect. With the warm-blooded bat the result was the same. And so he demonstrated precisely (and illustrated by personal drawings using his favourite aid, a camera lucida) the beginning of the phenomenon we call inflammation.

Below Lister's living model of inflammation. He has drawn the blood vessels in the web of a frog, as seen under the microscope. The bottom drawing shows how the vessels dilate after the application of heat. The black spots are the pigment cells of the frog skin.

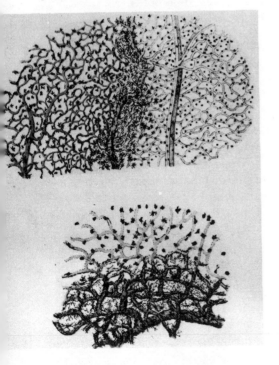

He was able to confirm what others had thought but as he said "No-one has, I believe, hitherto told the tale as it ought to be told!".

Therefore he described clearly exactly what happens when an injury or wound occurs to the body. Each one of us can appreciate the redness and swelling and heat that occurs, say, after sunburn, or any burn, or any scratch or injury involving the skin. It is how our body responds.

It is said that if only Lister had waited for a few more hours of those glorious nights (and this would have meant no sleep at all) he would have observed the white cells of the blood begin to move like amoebae through the walls of the capillaries to join up with other cells, to act as scavengers to clear away any dead cells and debris caused by the injury. The migration of these white cells was described later by Professor Cohnheim in 1867, and the scavenging action by Professor Metchnikoff in 1883. Finally, if he had waited days longer he would have seen how cells

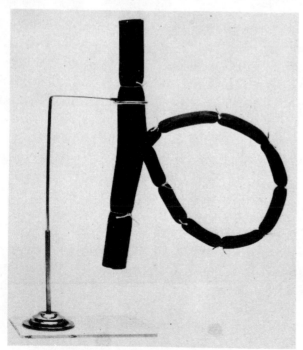

Left An example of Lister's experimental technique. This experiment was designed to test the theory that blood outside the body coagulated because of the escape of ammonia.

The rubber tube was inserted into the jugular vein of a sheep in such a way that the blood flowed through the tube and then continued its natural course. While the blood was circulating the tube was tied into a number of airtight receptacles containing blood. The blood in these receptacles was examined after various intervals of time.

Lister found that the blood coagulated in these receptacles (although they did not allow for the escape of ammonia) as quickly as in those which were open to the air. He concluded that the escape of ammonia was not one of the causes that brought about coagulation of the blood.

of the body start the process of repair by producing a substance called collagen (a kind of chemical darning-material of nature).

As a by-product of these observations he solved the problem of why the skin of a frog may change colour according to environment (like a chameleon). He found it was not due to expansion or contraction of the pigment cells but due to a movement of pigment inside the cells.

And for all this work done in the "glorious nights", and the papers which were written and published and presented to scientists, he was elected a Fellow of the Royal Society in 1860. Like Dr. Edward Jenner before him, this honour was given for scientific work done before the great discovery. (In Jenner's case it was work on the baby cuckoo and not his later work on vaccination.)

In later years Lister went on to study the reason why the blood should clot (coagulate), and although many more factors in clotting have been discovered

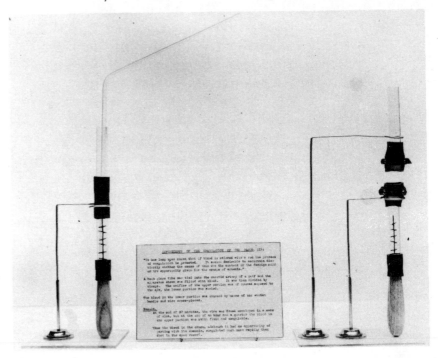

Right A further experiment on the coagulation of blood. One sample was open to the air, thus allowing the escape of ammonia, whilst the other was churned with a small wire paddle. The blood being churned coagulated far more quickly.

Lister was able to conclude that contact with a foreign solid (in this case, the wire paddle) was an important cause of coagulation.

since his day, he was the man who so carefully demonstrated that damage to the lining of the blood vessels plays an important part in causing the blood to clot. Many scientists today repeat his experiment to provide what is called a "model", in order that they may test the action of drugs used to treat either clotting of blood or early inflammation due to any cause.

And so, by the time he left Edinburgh in 1860 to become Regius Professor of Surgery in Glasgow, he had accomplished what today is still of great importance for surgeons in training. He had undergone a period of training in the service of patients (care and operations) and had spent time on a project which could be used to help reduce suffering and disease. He had to spend one "glorious night" after another, working until the early hours of the morning in order to get results.

His original work on the beginning of inflammation was very much related to the problems of wound infection in hospitals. The phenomenon of inflammation can occur without infection, but it is always more severe when there is infection with bacteria. Sometimes inflammation runs riot due to overwhelming infection, when the blood clots and the blood vessels become blocked and the flesh rots under the attack of bacteria. This is what Lister had to face. He saw that inflammation was running riot in the hospital patients with wound infection, but why did it get out of hand? No-one knew then that it was due to bacterial invasion. At least with his scientific experience Lister's mind was prepared—prepared for the leap in the dark, the crucial experiment which was to suggest itself in 1865.

6 *The Problem and the Experiment*

When Lister moved from Edinburgh to Glasgow in 1860 to become Regius Professor of Surgery, the first year was spent in teaching students and continuing his research on inflammation caused by injury. There were a lot of students with a particular respect for learning and they soon appreciated their young professor, for he seemed to be bringing a new look into surgery. They gave him support in getting beds in the hospital so that he could treat patients and

Below Lister always inspired great friendship and loyalty in his students and nursing staff. This picture shows him, some thirty years after he first became a Professor, on a ward at King's College Hospital, London.

practise properly as a surgeon, performing operations. In other words he was able to do what is called clinical work.

Immediately, Lister would have realized that he had now accepted a special responsibility. There was no Professor Syme at hand to ask for guidance or on whom to rest a patient's future. He, Lister, was the only one to decide exactly how his patients should be treated. They would look to him for help—there would be no-one else. Using a modern phrase we would say "the buck stopped with Lister".

Every failure of a treatment to relieve suffering was, to a surgeon with such an upbringing and training as Lister had, a serious defeat. He wanted so much to introduce and extend the new operations he had so carefully planned, but he dare not. Any patient with a broken bone (a fracture) which punctured the skin, or any flesh wound, or a burn, or an abscess which needed operation, was in mortal peril. The chances of getting out of hospital alive after any kind of treatment of wounds or after any operation were very slender. It was a 50/50 chance after, say, removal of a leg (amputation), and in some hospitals the chances were less than this.

And why was there such a danger? We, today, know the answer—infection by bacteria—but Lister and his world did not. They saw the effects, not knowing the cause. They had to stand and see the skin and flesh around wounds become intensely red and hot and swollen. This suppuration, as they called it, would get worse, the skin turning black with gangrene. Foul-smelling fluid and pus would run out of the patient due to the rottenness or putrefaction which seemed to be eating its way into the body. The blood would become full of poison (septicaemia), causing shivering, high fever, wasting of the whole body, which would end in death. The whole state of affairs they called "sepsis". It was indeed dreadful sepsis.

Above The title page of Lister's important paper explaining his new antiseptic treatment of compound fractures, abscesses, etc. The paper, written as a result of his work in Glasgow, was first published in *The Lancet* in March, 1867.

Day after day, year after year, the scene was the same: the dreadful sepsis went on. It had gone on for hundreds of years and surgeons had not only grown to accept it, but realised that their art was paralysed because of it. A great Russian surgeon, Pirogoff, once said it was just a matter of chance or luck if a patient survived an operation. Lister, too, knew that progress in surgery was paralysed by sepsis. Was there no way in which surgery could be made safe?

Lister certainly understood the early stages of inflammation because of his research. But what went wrong, why did inflammation get out of hand and run riot in the patient's body? The doctors and scientists of those days believed that putrefaction was due to the oxygen in the air. They believed that the flesh became oxidised. Accordingly, the surgeons invented types of dressings to wounds which would keep out the air. Professor Syme was keen on dry dressings of, say, linen, though they soon became soaked with blood and pus. Professor Liston, who had years before moved from Edinburgh to work in University College Hospital, London, and was one of Lister's teachers, believed in water dressings and immersing the wounds in baths of water. Surely water over a wound would keep the air out and prevent this dreadful form of sepsis?

Like others, Lister had tried both methods of dressing without success. Yet he, like the others, felt that the problem must be something to do with the air because, if the skin is unbroken, the body is protected. Furthermore he noticed that even if the skin were broken the formation of a good hard scab, such as he observed in animals and also in children, also gave some protection.

And there were other ideas about the cause of sepsis. Sir John Ericksen, another of Lister's teachers, said the trouble was in the very bricks and mortar of a hospital—he called it "hospitalism"—and that the only solution was to pull down all the old hospitals and build new ones which in their turn would have to be replaced. Lister certainly had cause to worry about possible "hospitalism". Not only were his patients crowded together, but he found "a multitude of coffins" just below the surface of the ground, four feet from his ward, containing the bodies from a cholera epidemic in 1849. Also nearby was a city burial pit for paupers, barely covered over. This was the environment in which Lister had to do his work. So he cleaned up his ward and did something about the overcrowding, but this, though a

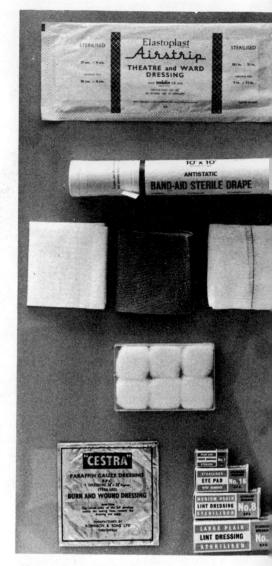

Above A selection of modern surgical dressings that all follow Lister's principle of antisepsis. They stop infection from reaching the wound and, therefore, prevent sepsis.

48

helpful step against the spread of infection, did not solve the real problem.

Now a university should be a place where scientists working in all kinds of subjects can get together and talk about their projects and problems. Sometimes a chance remark by a doctor of medicine will help an engineer or a physicist and vice versa. In this case chemistry helped surgery. Let us imagine that Lister is talking to Dr. Thomas Anderson, Professor of Chemistry, about the awful problem of hospital sepsis and how far he has got with his thinking about the cause. Anderson ponders and then says, "There's a chemist in France, called Louis Pasteur, who is writing in a chemistry journal about his proof that there are living things in the air—

Below Louis Pasteur in his laboratory at the Ecole Normale, Paris.

microbes—germs—'vibrios'—which cause fermentation and putrefaction. He is saying putrefaction is not spontaneous, and is not due to oxygen, or the air itself."

We can imagine how this remark was received in Lister's prepared and receptive mind. And, after all, did not Pasteur say "Chance favours the prepared mind"?

While it took others so many years to understand Pasteur's work, Lister saw immediately that Pasteur could be right, his experiments being simple, reproducible and conclusive. Lister was able to follow the method and reproduce the same result (Chapter 3). The next step or leap in Lister's thoughts was that if yeasts or as yet unseen germs in the air could cause fermentation and, therefore, putrefaction, they might be the cause of wound suppuration and sepsis. And, if Pasteur could kill such microbial life by heat, some way might be found to kill or prevent this form of life attacking his patients. Heat was impractical. Again Dr Anderson helped Lister.

In 1834 a man called Runge discovered a chemical called carbolic acid and it was available in a crude form known as creosote. It was found to be useful in stopping the rotting of wood used for railway sleepers and for ships, and for preventing decomposition. An English chemist, Calvert, began to manufacture carbolic acid in a fairly pure form in 1857. Lister, in 1865, read that carbolic acid was being used to control the decomposition of sewage in Carlisle, and thought that if it prevented decomposition it might prevent or cure wound sepsis. It might be truly anti septic. Dr. Anderson gave him some of the crude carbolic acid, known as German creosote.

Now Lister had to look for an opportunity to try the experiment. He wanted to use carbolic acid in dressings for patients who were most likely to get wound suppuration. It would be meaningless if he tried it on a strong, well-nourished, young patient

Above Carbolic acid was the first chemical Lister used in antisepsis.

with a trivial injury. That would not prove anything. In March, 1865, he selected a man with a severe injury and a broken leg. Alas, the carbolic acid which he had put in the dressing did not work and the man died. Lister, distressed and disappointed as he must have been, still believed he was on the right track. Then a boy, aged eleven, was admitted. He had been run over by a cart. Both legs were broken, and also the skin. Lister told his house surgeon to dip a piece of lint into the carbolic acid and to cover the wound completely with it. The fractures were reduced (i.e. the bones were set) and the legs were put into splints. At first all seemed well, but on the fourth day the wound became painful and Lister began to think the worst had happened. He removed the dressing and found that all was well. A good scab had formed, there was no suppuration and the cause of the pain was due to the burning of the skin by the crude carbolic. Another carbolic dressing was applied and the wound proceeded to heal well and the boy recovered. However, Lister felt that perhaps the boy might have recovered after all, without the carbolic acid dressing. One possible "favourable case" was no proof.

By the beginning of 1867 Lister had collected thirteen examples of compound fracture treated by this new method. The first case had died. The third, while doing very well initially, got hospital gangrene while Lister was away from Glasgow. Lister resolved that he would have to do the dressings himself if he was going to find out if carbolic acid provided the answer to his hypothesis. There were some of these cases which he thought might have healed well anyway ("favourable cases"). But there were seven cases of severe injury which would have needed amputation with all its dreadful consequences. All seven did well without suppuration. It was quite "abnormal", unusual in fact, for such good results to be obtained. Lister, therefore, wrote a paper on all these cases, together with other cases of abscess treated equally suc-

i.e as if there were
no wound. And 12
days have now elapsed
since the accident.
If the case continues
to do well to a cure, I
certainly hope to
publish it, as it would
in that case, sufficiently
prove in itself that this
new mode of treatment
is valuable.
With our united dear
love to all
  I remain
    They own affect son
      Joseph Lister

cessfully, and the paper was published in the medical journal *The Lancet* in March and April, 1867.

Throughout his trial of this new treatment using this new idea of antisepsis he kept his former teacher and father-in-law, Professor Syme, informed, and especially wrote to his father:

May 27th, 1866
"There is one of my cases at the Infirmary which I am sure will interest thee. It is one of compound fracture of the leg; with a wound of considerable size . . . . Though hardly expecting success, I tried the application of carbolic acid to the wound, to prevent decomposition of the blood, and so avoid the fearful mischief of suppuration throughout the limb. Well, it is now 8 days since the accident and the patient has been going on exactly as if there were no external wound . . . there is no appearance of any matter forming."

June 3rd.
". . . the original crust of clotted blood, lint and carbolic acid . . . still remains without a drop of matter (pus)."

June 11th.
"I have a continued good report to give of the compound fracture which is indeed now no longer a case of uncertainty. . . ."

And so, on that first great success in an unfavourable case and the six similar cases that were to follow, Lister laid the foundations on which to build the future of surgery.

7 Dressings, The Spray, Surgical Materials

Dressings

As soon as he found that carbolic acid was effective, Lister started to devise the best kind of dressing. This work took many years, and improvements came about by trial and error. First of all he had to obtain pure carbolic acid crystals as the crude German creosote burnt the skin. But pure carbolic could also do harm so it had to be diluted. If water was used to dilute the acid only about six per cent was soluble, and this was not always enough to be effective. As the acid would dissolve in oil, various kinds of oil were used such as linseed oil, and eventually paraffin oil and a resin.

Below Lister's impregnated carbolic dressing.

Below Blow-up of a very similar modern surgical dressing which follows the same antiseptic principle.

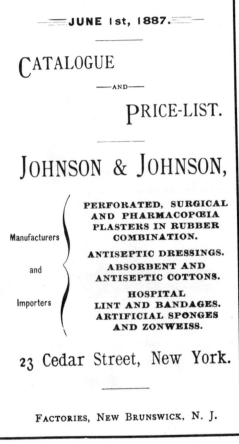

Above The title page from the first catalogue of Johnson & Johnson, the large American medical dressing manufacturers. The company was formed in 1886 to manufacture antiseptic dressings.

He was sure that his dressing should mimic as far as possible a scab, nature's second-best to skin as a protection against germs (bacteria). He had to invent a dressing which could be moulded to any particular curve of the body—i.e. it had to be flexible. Putty, gutta percha, and then resin and oil answered this purpose. It was also necessary that the carbolic acid should be retained in the dressing and not diluted or washed out by any discharges. Carbolic acid in an oily base was again most suitable. Furthermore the putty or resin containing the carbolic should not stick to the skin, and discharges had to be absorbed by the dressing.

He hunted around linen shops and decided that a dressing made up of layers of muslin was best. (Muslin or cotton gauze is used to this day.) Then, knowing that a scab does not let in any fluid or air, he experimented by inserting a layer of metal foil and oiled silk. Later he found that thin macintosh, which was in use then for hat lining, was very effective. It used to be dyed pink so that people would know which was the outside of the dressing.

He found that it was necessary to keep the dressings damp in a box, to stop evaporation of the carbolic acid. When he used them he always put a few layers of gauze soaked in carbolic solution next to the wound in order to be on the safe side.

Naturally he became interested in other antiseptic chemicals besides carbolic acid. Other surgeons were trying salicylic acid and boracic acid. Provided they killed bacteria and did not harm the patient they would be suitable. Lister developed the use of salts of heavy metals such as mercury and zinc. He was to find mercury perchloride (corrosive sublimate) very effective and then the double cyanide of mercury and zinc. The gauze dressing containing this chemical was coloured mauve and it became popular because it did not irritate the skin and could

Left T J Smith, the founder of the medical dressing company, Smith & Nephew Limited. The company is still one of the major dressing manufacturers in Britain.

Top right The carbolic spray apparatus.

be used with carbolic lotion as well.

Of course the demand for these dressings increased as Lister's ideas were accepted. Companies were formed to manufacture dressings in Britain by Mr. Robinson of Chesterfield, T J Smith of London, and in the USA by R W Johnson of Philadelphia. Other antiseptic products were made, for example, dog soap, but they were just disinfectant "lines" and were not, of course, related to the principle that Lister was so intent on. Lister must have been very upset whenever he saw his name used on these brands.

Bottom right Operating with Lister's antiseptic carbolic spray, c. 1875.

56

The Spray

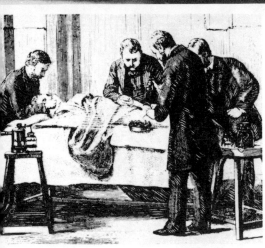

Lister seems to be remembered most for his antiseptic carbolic spray. In fact he regretted ever having invented it. Yet it was a necessary development of his idea of using a chemical to prevent germs getting into wounds during operations. For he knew that Pasteur was right and that carbolic acid in dressings prevented or overcame sepsis. It followed that a fine spray of carbolic acid in the air around the patient during the operation was bound to be of help.

He invented different kinds of machine with which

to spray carbolic acid. The principle was the same in each. Air, under pressure generated by a hand pump, or steam generated under pressure by boiling water, was used to draw carbolic acid from a container to form a mist, in the same way as a simple fly spray works. The smaller hand pump was operated by squeezing an india rubber ball. It was tiring to use, so a larger long-handled bellows affair was made, nicknamed the "donkey engine".

The steam-operated sprays were much more effective, though they did not always work properly. Also the spray was not without danger of damage to sensitive membranes in the patients and the surgeons. For example, Queen Victoria complained to her physician, Sir William Jenner, of the stinging it caused in her eyes when Lister was opening the abscess under her arm. Sir William apologised, "I'm afraid, Ma'am, I'm only the man who is working the machine."

Finally, when it was realized that carbolic acid could actually cause damage internally, and when it was found that germs (bacteria) could be spread by water or by any dirt on the hands or instruments, the spray was abandoned. Gradually other chemical, physical and engineering methods were adopted to exclude bacteria from wounds, measures which were given the name "aseptic" instead of "antiseptic". We, who are carefully following Lister's story, realize that there is really little difference in the meaning of these words. Lister knew he had to exclude germs by interposing a chemical barrier to their entry into the body. Today we still use chemicals, and also heat and special techniques to exclude this bacterial contamination (Chapter 10).

Surgical Materials. Silk, Catgut, Wire

While Lister's first great experiment was to introduce carbolic acid into dressings to act as a barrier to the

Below Lister's own drawing of a catgut ligature which was removed from a patient some days after an operation in 1869. It can be seen that a part of the ligature has dissolved away harmlessly within the patient. Lister's note on the picture reads: "Cat gut ligature prepared by steeping for a month in watery solution of carbolic acid 1 to 20: removed seven days after introduction into the integument of the chest, after removal of the mamma." [i.e. the breast]. The drawing has been magnified by the camera lucida which Lister frequently used.

germs in the air, he was obviously receptive to the work of men like Professor Burdon Sanderson who found that germs can be spread by water or any other fluid or medium. He reasoned that any material or instrument used in an operation should first be soaked in an antiseptic. He had an idea which proved to be of great importance in the story of how modern surgery began. We can only understand this idea if we know a particular detail of every surgical operation.

In any operation a surgeon has to cut across the arteries and veins of his patient. The loss of blood is stopped by applying a special kind of forceps and then by tying the blood vessel with silk or linen thread and removing the forceps. These threads are a kind of fine string and are called ligatures. If they are used to join together parts of the body, such as intestine or skin, they are called sutures. Before the time of Lister's next experiment it was always necessary to tie the knot and to leave the long ends of the ligature hanging out of the wound. When inflammation and sepsis occurred, the ligature would become free and could be removed. Unfortunately, on account of infection, the blood clot in the artery might not be firm, and dangerous bleeding (secondary haemorrhage) would follow, from which the patient might die.

It seems unbelievable today that these ligatures of silk or linen were undone and used again and again in different patients. They were carried around by the young doctors and students (dressers) in the buttonholes of their coats and handed to the surgeon when he called for one during an operation. Blood and pus were dried on and in them. The bloodier they were the more daring and famous the surgeon was supposed to be.

We, of course, know that those re-used ligatures were spreading infection from one patient to another. Only one person before Lister had realized how disease such as hospital infection could be carried from

59

one patient to another by dirty hands. He was a Hungarian called Dr Semmelweis. He tried to get people to wash their hands in a solution containing chlorine, for by attention to cleanliness he could reduce the incidence of childbed fever and the deaths it caused. Few would believe him and he died, after an unhappy life, from blood poisoning due to infection in 1865, the year of Lister's antiseptic discovery. Lister, at that time, had not heard of this other great pioneer in the battle against disease, death and human prejudice.

Lister planned his experiment. He soaked the silk ligature in a solution of carbolic acid. On the 12th December, 1867, he operated on a horse and tied an artery and cut the ends of the ligature short. He applied an antiseptic dressing. The wound healed with-

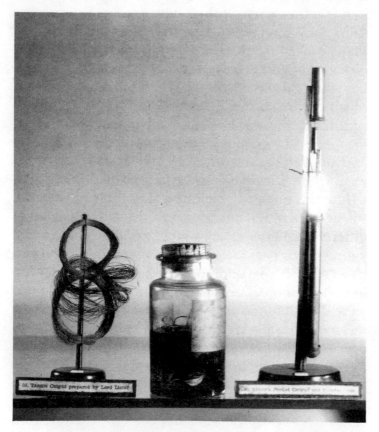

Left The picture shows (far left) catgut sterilized in tannin by Lister; weighted catgut in an antiseptic solution (centre); and (near left) Lister's pocket case in which he carried ready-sterilized catgut.

Below The production of sterilized ligatures was quickly taken over by commercial manufacturers.

out any suppuration. Six weeks later the old horse died and Lister took the opportunity to look at the ligature. The ligature was still there; it had not come undone and there was no suppuration.

Lister wasted no time in trying this new idea on a patient. A woman, aged fifty-one, a private patient, was suffering from an aneurysm of the thigh. An aneurysm is a bulging artery due to weakness of its wall and there is the danger of it rupturing (bursting) and the patient bleeding to death. Lister repeated his experiment, tying off the artery and cutting the ligature short and closing the wound. Healing was immediate, by what is called "first intention". He wrote to his father, "I don't think any case ever excited me so much . . . ." The patient remained well for ten months then died suddenly from the bursting of another aneurysm inside her body. Lister was able to make an examination of his ligature in the thigh, and found that it had remained secure and had caused little reaction.

No wonder he was excited. From that moment on he was able to perform old and new operations with much greater safety. At first he had to prepare his own materials. He found that the concentration of carbolic acid solution kept in a bottle was not uniform if it was allowed to stand. It was too weak near the surface of the fluid. So he put weights on the coils of silk to keep them on the bottom of the bottle. In this way he rendered the silk germ-free. He was, in fact, carrying out chemical sterilization of the silk.

Then he tried out this method of sterilizing ligatures on another kind of ligature material called catgut, which had long been in use for stringing violins and cellos. The gut is not obtained from cats, but from the intestine of sheep. Probably it was called after a country name for a violin—a "kit". In the days when pedlars went from village to village their kit was kept with all their wares in a "kit bag", also sewn together with this gut.

One can imagine the dangerous germs there could be in catgut, particularly the tetanus germ which causes lockjaw, nearly always a fatal infection. Lister tried carbolized catgut in an operation on a calf and reported his success to his father, including the fact that catgut appeared to blend with the body and leave little trace. What a great step forward it was, a ligature which would do its job of stopping bleeding and then disappear after a week or so.

But the process of preparation of sterilized catgut was slow. Some surgeons used imperfectly sterilized gut and cases of tetanus occurred. Lister, while content with good-quality gut, carefully prepared, examined other ways of sterilization, using iodine, tannin and, finally, mercury perchloride (corrosive sublimate) with chromium sulphate. This "chromic" gut was strong and did not disappear so quickly as plain catgut so it became very popular for sewing intestines together. Today it is still very much in use. Great industries have taken over its preparation, as well as other ligature materials like silk, nylon, etc., under the strict quality control required by law.

Naturally Lister turned his attention to the use of wire, such as silver wire, to rejoin broken bones (fractures). The first operation was to unite a fractured knee-cap (patella). Fortunately for him it was successful (Chapter 8). Immediately the treatment of fractured bones underwent a revolution and Lister and then other surgeons used long pegs of ivory or steel, or plates and screws.

To be able safely to place within the body foreign materials, providing they had been sterilized by a chemical, was to signal to the world of surgery a great "GO AHEAD!" The lights were green at last.

All the modern spare-part surgery of today with artificial joints, heart valves and blood vessels, stems from those experiments with antiseptics on silk, catgut and wire.

Below Lister's ivory and steel bone nails.

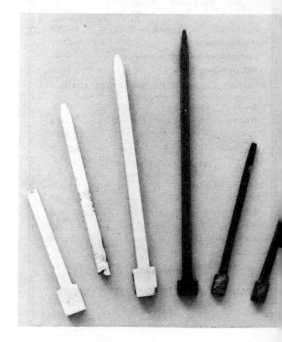

Rubber Drainage Tubes

There is yet another innovation of Lister's to be recalled, and Queen Victoria herself was the first patient in this new experiment. It was at the time in Balmoral (1871) that Lister operated on that abscess in the armpit. He made his incision and let out the pus of the abscess, perhaps stretching the opening with those long dressing forceps of his, since called sinus forceps. But the Queen did not get better. The abscess stopped draining through the wick of lint he had inserted. The tension of the pus built up again. Lister

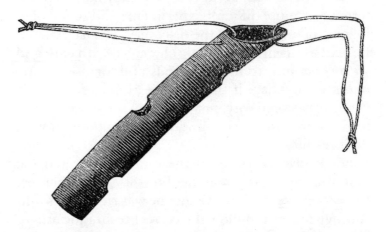

Right A rubber drainage tube. Lister first used one on Queen Victoria. Similar drainage tubes are still used by surgeons today (see the picture on page 88).

took a walk in the grounds of Balmoral to think over this difficult problem. Suddenly the thought occurred to him that he could keep the abscess draining properly if he inserted a piece of india rubber tubing with holes cut in the side. So he cut off a piece of the tubing of the carbolic spray, soaked it in carbolic overnight and inserted it into the abscess, with immediate success. Unknown to Lister, a French surgeon had already introduced drainage tubes made from bone, but it was Lister, with his royal patient, who made the surgical world aware of the value of the rubber tube drain, and contributed in this way to the relief of suffering and the saving of lives.

8 Disbelief and Acclaim

It is easy for us today, using the modern microscope and knowing the ways of growing and identifying bacteria by culture, to take sides with Lister against his opponents. He believed in Pasteur's germ theory of fermentation and putrefaction and how it related to the problem of hospital infection; they did not. He reproduced Pasteur's simple experiment, following the directions with great care, but they made up different and more difficult experiments and so failed to follow and understand the discovery. He used carbolic acid as his first antiseptic chemical, with care and with precision, to dress wounds and for use during operations. They, if they tried it at all, used it in a vague occasional way, not using it in the sense of antisepsis—against sepsis—and were disappointed with their results.

For twelve years, from the time he collected the first thirteen cases together in 1867 (Chapter 6), Lister persevered to prove that he was right and to encourage others to follow the correct technique and to find out that surgery could be made safer. During these years he moved, with his good tidings, from Glasgow to Edinburgh. He might never have moved to London in 1877 had the surgeons there not been the most resistant of all to his discovery. He was happy in Edinburgh where he had many patients, good wards, adoring students, and colleagues whom he had been able to convince. London was bigger—the hub of the world—and Lister, who after all was born a Londoner and had been a London medical student, believed he had a mission. Some said he believed it was a divinely-inspired mission. He knew his work could not be accomplished unless it was accepted there.

Right Lister's portable medicine chest.

Although attacks on Lister and the good news from converts at home and abroad occurred at one and the same time, it is probably best to recall first the attacks, and then to relate the good news as it came in. The attacks took on a form similar to that mounted against most discoveries:

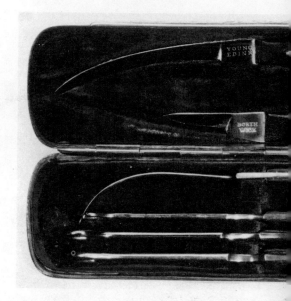

1. Disbelief in the basic idea that microbes, as deduced by Pasteur as the cause of fermentation, were the cause of hospital infection. It was a lot of nonsense.
2. It was not a new idea. Others had tried carbolic acid before and it had been discarded.
3. It had to be tested by comparing results between patients treated, and with patients not treated by Lister's methods, i.e. statistical proof was required.
4. It challenged the ideas of others who were working along different lines.
5. Envy or jealousy, particularly because of Lister's relative youthfulness. Many were incensed by Lister's occasional sanctimonious behaviour, his quiet, grave manner, never losing his temper, giving long sighs over the tiresome disbelief of his opponents. He seemed imperturbable, and so sure of his discovery.

It must be remembered that those who challenged him were not bad men, they were good doctors and surgeons at the top of their profession. Most in their time had had to learn to accept the awful horror of hospital infection and they had to develop their own ways and means of coping under the circumstances. After many years of effort they were bound to find it difficult to believe in a cause of disease which they could neither see nor touch. A good example was Professor Sir James Young Simpson of Edinburgh.

Simpson had discovered the value of chloroform as an anaesthetic in 1847. He, like other great discoverers, had had to endure attack and scorn until

Above Lister's surgical
instruments in their carrying case.

the world realized that he had done something to
relieve the suffering of humanity. Surely he, of all
people, would have been the first to understand and
support this new Professor. But no, he thought
Pasteur's work nonsense, and how on earth could a
chemical like carbolic acid change the course of disease? Probably there were two reasons for his opposition. Firstly, here was a young surgeon who seemed
to challenge his own place as a discoverer, and
secondly he himself had been working for some time
on the problem of hospital infection.

Simpson, like every good surgeon, was appalled at
the results of surgery, especially after amputation of
the leg, and had collected the statistics on the death
rate from many hospitals. He, like Lister and others,
had noticed the increased chances of complications
when the ligatures (Chapter 7) used for tying the
arteries and veins were left hanging out of the
wounds. There was indeed something awful about
them which sowed the seed of trouble. But, because
he did not accept Pasteur's germ theory, he missed a
good opportunity to do what Lister did with his ligatures—sterilize them with an antiseptic chemical.

Simpson thought that the way to stop suppuration
of the wound after amputation was to do away with
ligatures and to arrest bleeding by the use of long
needles pushed into the leg and positioned and
twisted in such a way as to compress the blood vessels. The needles were pulled out some days after the
operation when the blood had clotted firmly. The
method was called acupressure. It was a good idea,
but very limited in the way it could be used for all
kinds of operation, chiefly because it was based upon
ignorance of the real cause of hospital infection.

Then there was Dr Bennett, Professor of Medicine
in Edinburgh, who was an expert with the microscope. He disbelieved Pasteur because he could not
see any microbes, either in wine or wounds. "Show us
these germs and we will believe", he would say. "Has

67

Left A photograph of Lister some years after the medical world had finally accepted his antiseptic system. The picture was taken in about 1887, when he was aged 60.

anybody seen these germs?", and many other humorous but disparaging remarks. When he tried to reproduce Pasteur's work he did not perform the simple experiment with heated broth in a heated flask with a bent-over neck, but invented a complicated air filtration system which actually allowed germs to leak in and to contaminate. And so he caused putrefaction and did not hinder it. Therefore, not knowing his experiment was faulty, he did not believe in the germ theory of putrefaction. He thought he had done his best to exclude germs and did not know why he had failed.

There were many other opponents in England and France who disbelieved Pasteur and the reason why carbolic acid might work. It was mainly opposition by argument, and not by experience, and not even because of faulty experimental technique.

Eventually Lister was challenged by a surgeon, Mr. Savory, to reveal figures comparing results of operations with and without carbolic acid. It was a proper challenge and today the value of any new drug or operation would have to be tested against "controls" of the same age who are not receiving the treatment, and modern statistical tests would be applied. But Lister was, after all, working with a basic principle of nature and his improved results were highly suggestive from the start (Chapter 6). He felt that, as his surgery was already emerging from the dark cloud of sepsis into the sunlight of future surgery, it would not be proper, indeed it would be unethical, to return to the dark ages of the old surgery. He had kept very careful notes about each case, and later his assistants collected and published the figures proving the success of antisepsis.

His local colleagues in Glasgow and then in Edinburgh were soon won over. But it was the surgeons from abroad, especially in Denmark and Germany, who provided his critics with overwhelming experience and evidence that the antiseptic principle of preventing and treating wounds really worked.

Professor Saxtorph of Copenhagen came early and revisited his new-found surgeon friend. After giving the antiseptic method a careful trial for a year he felt it his duty to write a testimony in the form of a letter, which Lister then published in the medical press. Formerly Saxtorph had the old trouble with deaths caused by sepsis; now he had none. All the cases of compound fracture had healed without difficulty. All the amputations had recovered.

Saxtorph was followed by many famous German surgeons who had carefully followed Lister's directions—Nussbaum, Volkmann, Bardeleben, Thiersch, Hagedorn, Schönbarn, Schade and Langenbeck. As Nussbaum said, "There was one voice—that of praise . . . they could not find words enough to tell of the good of it."

Take Professor Nussbaum's experience as an example. In 1872, twenty per cent of his cases were attacked by infective hospital gangrene, in 1873, fifty per cent, and in 1874 there were eighty per cent, the sepsis "gnawing at the wound like a wild animal". The wards were called "lightly concealed graves".

Nussbaum, a good and noble surgeon, was in such distress that he appealed to Lister and sent an assistant, Dr Lindpainter, to make a careful study of the technique being used in Edinburgh. With the usual German thoroughness Nussbaum applied it strictly to the patients in Munich, with immediate success.

In 1875, in a great address to the Congress of German surgeons, Nussbaum hailed Lister's great discovery:

"One has no use for any words but those of gratitude and admiration. . . . Look now at my sick wards, recently ravaged by death . . . I and my assistant and nurses are overwhelmed with joy and undertake all the extra trouble the treatment entails with the greatest zeal. The happiest mood possesses us, whilst before we went about with hanging heads. What wonders of conservative surgery has the future in store for us!"

By 1876 Nussbaum had collected and published his statistical evidence to support these good tidings.

Other surgeons had a similar story to tell and figures to go with it. Pirogoff, in Russia, was foremost in spreading the good news in his country, while even on the other side of the world antisepsis was being used with success by a doctor treating injured gold-diggers in New Zealand. In France and the United States of America acceptance was slow. But the evidence was becoming indisputable.

By the time Lister went to London in 1877 on what was really his special and final mission, the revolution in surgery had already begun elsewhere. Only a few surgeons in London had taken the trouble to find out and to use successfully the antiseptic technique. These were surgeons such as Dr Lichtenberg, a German surgeon working in a little hospital in Dalston in the East End of London, and Mr Berkeley Hill of Lister's old hospital, University College Hospital.

Fortunately there were wise and eminent doctors

Right Lister on a ward at King's College Hospital, London, where he became Professor of Surgery in 1877.

70

Above University College (on the left of the picture) and (right) University College Hospital, in 1840. Lister began his medical training there in 1848. Mr Berkeley Hill, a surgeon at the hospital, was one of the first London surgeons to use Lister's antiseptic techniques.

in London who knew that Lister's presence in London was vital. They persuaded the Governors of King's College Hospital to allow Lister to become an extra Professor of Surgery and to bring a team of doctors and nurses with him from Edinburgh. Without men like Mr (later Sir) Watson Cheyne and Dr John Stewart, Lister knew he would have had a very difficult time. And it was difficult anyway. The team had few beds and no patients. The students were apathetic and only interested in cram courses to get through their examinations. They knew they would never be asked about any new-fangled ideas in an exam.

Dr Stewart wrote:

"We four unhappy men wandered about . . . and wondered why men did not open their eyes . . . the air was heavy with the odour of suppuration. The shining eye and flushed cheek spoke eloquently of surgical fever. We would show them how things should be done! But how? We had no patients!"

But in the space of two years, Lister succeeded. He convinced people by his ability to demonstrate the

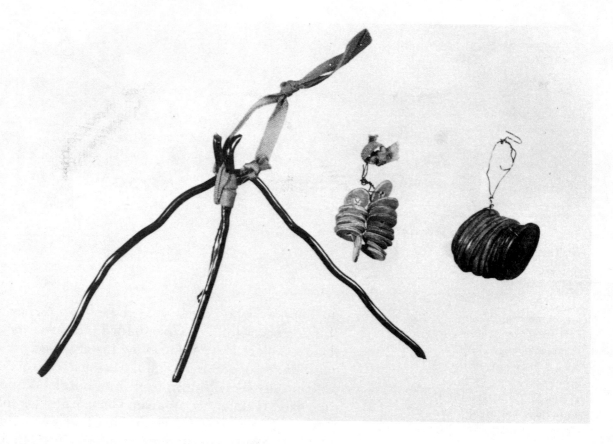

Pasteur experiments and his own work on milk, for he was a much sought-after lecturer. These lectures stimulated surgeons to send him difficult cases which no-one else would operate on. One patient had a cancer of the leg, thought to be quite untreatable. He removed the leg and two days later the patient was sitting up in bed without pain or fever, reading a newspaper. Another case was sent from a great London hospital where two of the finest surgeons refused to operate because of the risk of a large wound ending with hospital gangrene. This, too, Lister dealt with safely.

He was also able to show that it was possible to leave silver wire inside a patient who had broken his knee cap (patella). Anyone trying to wire the broken pieces together without the antiseptic technique would be faced with an infected knee and hospital gangrene. On hearing about this new operation, one surgeon exclaimed: "When the poor fellow dies, someone ought to proceed against that man (Lister) for malpractice!" But all went well and there was no infection.

At last the good news began to travel fast around London. Surgeons at King's College Hospital and others came to Lister to learn the technique and immediately the results of their surgery improved and they were soon able to devise new operations themselves to help cure disease.

There were one or two parting shots at Lister, misaimed and mistimed, rather mean and small. It was said repeatedly that Lister's work was not original, it was not a discovery. But Lister never claimed he had discovered the germ theory or even carbolic acid and its use as a disinfectant. Those who used carbolic acid in this way did not know exactly why it worked. Lister was the man who understood. If germs cause putrefaction, and if a chemical like carbolic acid stops putrefaction, then carbolic acid kills germs. Therefore, its constant use in and after operating will prevent and cure hospital sepsis.

1879 is reckoned to be the year of final acceptance of antisepsis. This was the year when Lister addressed five hundred surgeons and doctors from all over Europe at the International Congress of Medical Science in Amsterdam. *The British Medical Journal* reported:

"The whole assembly rose to its feet . . . deafening and repeated rounds of cheers . . . acclamations renewed minute after minute . . . his name again and again shouted forth . . . remarkable scene—unprecedented in the history of medical science! Professor Donders, the President, takes Lister's hand! Professor Lister, it is not only our admiration which we offer to you; it is our gratitude, and that of the nations to which we belong!"

9 Honours and Great Occasions

After the Amsterdam Congress of 1879 and the acceptance of antisepsis, honours began to be showered on Lister. It is said that he received them with mixed feelings, pleasure mixed with sadness. If only recognition had come sooner and antisepsis had been adopted earlier, much nearer to 1867, many more lives in Britain and abroad would have been saved. He would remember especially those wounded in the Franco-Prussian war of 1870 when German surgeons had to stop operating completely because at one time every man died after operation. And ten thousand out of thirteen thousand French soldiers died from infection after amputation.

He took a special delight in the Orders of Dannebrog conferred on him, because the Danish Pro-

Below A scene from the Franco-Prussian War of 1870, showing transport of the wounded by river steamers to the Paris ambulances. Casualties were heavy. Lister was saddened that his antiseptic techniques were not used in the treatment of the wounded.

Above A portrait of Lord Lister presiding at the Royal Society. He was elected President in 1895.

fessor Saxtorph was amongst the first to adopt antisepsis (Chapter 8). He received many gold medals and one supposes they were cherished with those he won in the University of London when he was a student. Among these new honours were the gold medal and the Copley medal of the Royal Society awarded for outstanding contributions to science. And there were gold medals from his surgical colleges, the Royal Colleges of Surgeons of England and Edinburgh, and from the Royal Institute of Public Health, the German Academy of Science, and the Society of Arts, Manufacturers and Commerce.

Diplomas awarded by universities and membership of medical and scientific academies and societies included those from Russia (Kiev), Germany (Bonn), Italy (Bologna) and from Belgium, France and Austria. In Rome a memorial sculptured frieze was raised above the entrance to the Royal Institute of Surgery.

Most of the treasures were eventually given, at Lister's bequest, to Edinburgh University for which Lister had a special affection. Amongst these and of special interest are the three caskets containing the "three freedoms" of the cities of Edinburgh (1898), London (1907) and Glasgow (1908). Another casket was presented by the University of Liverpool in 1898.

Added to these honours were those conferred by Queen Victoria and King Edward VII. In 1883 Queen Victoria conferred on him a baronetcy, making him Sir Joseph, and in 1897 (Queen Victoria's Diamond Jubilee year) she made him Lord Lister of Lyme Regis (where he, at one time, had a house). Lord Lister was, in fact, the first doctor to become a Peer of the House of Lords. Later, in 1902, King Edward VII included Lister in the first group of distinguished men to be appointed to the Order of Merit. He was also sworn in as a Privy Councillor.

All these honours, together with many honorary degrees from universities at home and abroad,

Below The casket of the Freedom of the City of London, presented to Lister on the 28th June, 1907.

marked the recognition and gratitude of the world.

There were many special occasions when acclamation was possible in an open and publicly joyful fashion. The extraordinary scenes which took place in Amsterdam in 1879 have already been reported (Chapter 8). Four years previously a similar tour had been made of German university towns, which involved many speeches and banquets and even performing an operation. In Berlin, Professor Langenbeck performed his first antiseptic operation in front of Lister.

In 1876 Lister had the opportunity to spread his good news across the Atlantic at an International Congress in Philadelphia. His words did not fall upon deaf ears, and included in the audience was H W Johnson who, realizing the value of Lister's work, was to develop his great dressing manufacturing company.

In May, 1897, when Lister was made a Peer, a banquet was held in his honour by 130 of the house surgeons who had served under him in Glasgow, Edinburgh and London. They wished to pay personal homage to, and acknowledge the pride they had in, the man that they always knew as "The Chief". By this time the sonnet "The Chief" by a former grateful patient in Edinburgh, W E Henley, was well-known.

"His brow spreads large and placid, and his eye
Is deep and bright, with steady looks that still.
Soft lines of tranquil thought his face fulfill—
His face at once benign and proud and shy.
If envy scout, if ignorance deny,
His faultless patience, his unyielding will,
Beautiful gentleness, and splendid skill,
Innumerable gratitudes reply.
His wise, rare smile is sweet with certainties,
And seems in all his patients to compel
Such love and faith as failure cannot quell.
We hold him for another Herakles,
Battling with custom, prejudice, disease,
As once the son of Zeus with Death and Hell."

Naturally the occasions when Lister and Pasteur were together were the most meaningful. Although the link between these two began in 1865, and they corresponded over Lister's work on the milk bacteria (Chapter 3), they did not meet until 1881 at a Congress in London. Lister gave a dinner of welcome to Pasteur. But the greatest occasion was in Paris in 1892, to celebrate Pasteur's seventieth birthday. Before an enormous audience in the Sorbonne, Lister presented an address to Pasteur from the Royal Societies of London and Edinburgh and Pasteur came forward to embrace Lister in the centre of the platform.

Pasteur's address, read to the Congress by his son, included immortal words:

Below Lord Lister (seated) being congratulated by Virchow at the Charing Cross Hospital, on the occasion of the Huxley lectures in 1898. Professor Rudolf von Virchow was an eminent German pathologist who had long admired Lister's work, particularly on coagulation of the blood, as he himself made a lasting contribution in this field.

". . . Science and peace will triumph over ignorance and war, that men will unite not to destroy but to build up, and that the future will belong to those who have done most for suffering humanity. And here I appeal to you, my dear Lister, and to you all . . ."

In 1900 the leading scientists in France gave a banquet in honour of Lister. Dr Champonnière, a leading surgeon and ardent follower of Lister, said: "We can remember the miserable condition of surgery and how great was the mortality. Nelaton [a famous French surgeon] said that a statue of gold should be raised to the person who was able to prevent what we now know as sepsis. You, Sir, have deserved that statue!" Another said, "You have driven back death itself; because in all you have done you have only caused tears of joy and gratitude."

The echo of gratitude was again heard in 1902 at the banquet of the Royal Society in London in the speech by the American Ambassador: "My Lord, it is not a profession, it is not a nation, it is humanity itself which with uncovered head salutes you."

10 Lister at Work Today

Below An exhibit from the Lister Centenary Conference of 1967. (Lister's initial reports on the antiseptic technique were first published in 1867). The display shows the difference between dressings which allowed bacteria to reach a wound, causing sepsis, and those which absorb blood and discharges and contain a barrier to bacterial contamination and are antiseptic (see Chapters 6 and 7).

On the right of the picture is a licence for the manufacture of safe dressings. Below this are photographs of Colonel Robinson, T J Smith and General Johnson, the founders of three major companies which are still making dressings today.

In his later years Lord Lister was to see a new word "asepsis" begin to replace "antisepsis". Asepsis, popularised in England by such men as Lawson Tait of Birmingham, and in Germany by Von Bergmann, was based on the idea of excluding bacteria from any opening into the body made by a surgeon. It is a pity that this word was ever invented. Perhaps many people did not really understand that this was indeed the principle that Lister had discovered. His discovery was not a method of treatment; he had declared war on all bacteria which might cause infection in a wound. Rightly he called this war "anti sepsis", meaning "against sepsis". Therefore, any barrier, whether chemical (e.g. carbolic acid, iodine, mercury perchloride) or by heat, or by sterilized macintosh rubber or material of any kind is *anti*septic.

The main drawback of any chemical barrier used throughout an operation is that it is very irritant to

the patient, surgeon and nurses. In a concentrated form chemicals can be also downright dangerous and a cause of accidental poisoning. Pure carbolic acid has completely faded out of the hospital scene today.

It is very instructive to follow, step by step, a so-called "aseptic" operation of today in order to appreciate that Lister's antiseptic principle is still being followed. Let us take out somebody's appendix together, an operation known as appendicectomy and which is known in the USA as appendectomy.

First of all, just a little anatomy (study of structure) and pathology (study of disease) to remind us that the appendix is a part of the intestine which lies in the lower right hand side of the belly or abdomen (see drawing). It is a blind end, a cul-de-sac, sticking

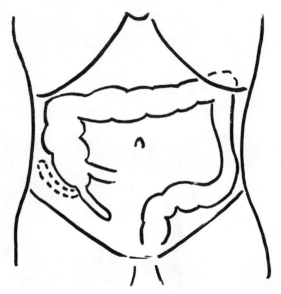

out like a worm just where the small intestine becomes the large intestine, at the caecum. Should the appendix become blocked and badly infected by bacteria, acute appendicitis will occur. The appendix then may burst (perforate) and pus and bacteria will flood the whole of the cavity of the abdomen (peritonitis). Let us assume that our patient has acute appendicitis and it is vital to remove the appendix lest such

Top right Preparations against sepsis—"scrubbing up". A member of the surgical team, wearing a cleanly laundered shirt, trousers, cap and mask, is washing and scrubbing his hands in running water, using an antiseptic chemical.

Left The anatomy of the appendix, caecum and large intestine. The dotted lines show another possible position of the appendix, behind or beside the caecum.

Bottom right Preparations against sepsis—putting on the sterilized gown. The nurse behind helps to fasten it. The colours of the uniforms and gowns vary according to fashion—white, grey, green and blue.

80

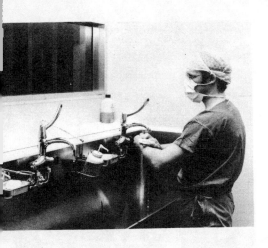

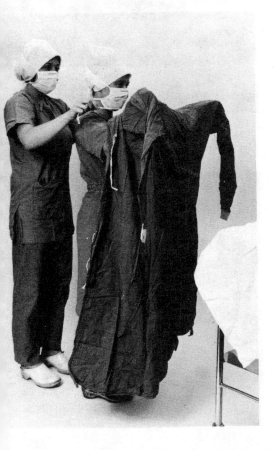

dangerous consequences arise. Let us begin the operation.

A modern type of anaesthetic has been given and the patient is now asleep and cannot feel any pain. The surgeon, assistants and nurses make their preparations. All will have changed from their everyday clothes into cleanly laundered shirts and trousers, or dresses. Clean rubber boots or clogs are worn instead of outdoor shoes. A cloth or paper hat covers the hair, and a special type of paper mask is worn over the nose and mouth. All these preparations are for the purpose of reducing the chance of bringing unwanted bacteria into the theatres from the wards and other parts of the hospital. They are preparations which produce the first barrier, the background of defence, against sepsis. Lister did not, in fact, appreciate the usefulness of these preparations as he relied almost solely on his chemical defence.

The next barrier against sepsis is the removal of and killing of bacteria on the hands by washing and using a scrubbing brush for the finger nails. The general rule is to wash and scrub with soap and running water for three to five minutes and an antiseptic chemical is commonly used at the same time, such as a chemical called chlorhexidine or a modern soapy form of iodine. Indeed we can remember in passing that the first space capsule to return from the moon was scrubbed with a similar iodine solution on landing, just in case any strange bacteria had been brought back from the moon.

From now on the operating team do not touch anything which has not been rendered germ-free (sterile), by either heat, or a chemical, or by atomic irradiation. Another barrier to infection is now put on, a linen gown with big sleeves which has been rendered free from germs (sterilized) by the most frequently used type of antiseptic, namely, heat. The heat is generated from steam under pressure in a special steel container called an "autoclave". It is of interest to note that Lister was one of the first to use a small autoclave (his iron "hot box") for his experiments with bacteria.

This leaves only the hands to be covered by fine rubber gloves which have been carefully sterilized by heat. The cuffs of these gloves have already been turned over by the manufacturers so it is possible to put them on without contaminating the outside of the rubber with the bare fingers. Should the gloves become punctured during an operation, they have to be changed. A surgical team may change into fresh gloves during an operation if there has been any chance of bacterial contamination.

Lister and the surgeons of his day did not use rubber gloves. As a result they suffered from sore,

Top right Preparations against sepsis—the autoclave, a modern version of Lister's hot box. The instruments ready for sterilizing are on shelves or hooks.

Bottom right Preparation against sepsis—putting on the sterile rubber gloves.

chapped hands. The irritation of the skin was made worse when corrosive sublimate (mercury perchloride) was used as the antiseptic for sterilizing the instruments. The instrument nurses suffered particularly. A famous American surgeon, Professor Halstead, asked a rubber company to make some protective gloves for his nurses, and this was the reason why gloves were used in the first place. Today the preparation of the hands still depends principally upon the careful washing and use of an antiseptic chemical before the gloves are put on. It is dangerous to rely on gloves alone.

The instrument nurse lays out the trolley for the instruments and ligatures. Beforehand the trolley will have been washed (swabbed) with an antiseptic

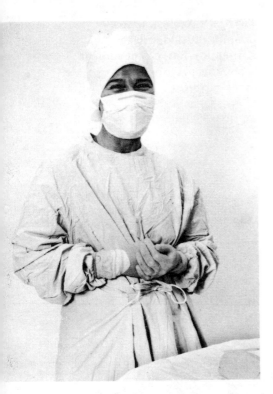

Above   The instrument nurse is ready. In this picture she is wearing a grey gown.

chemical. On it will be placed a sterilized macintosh or paper barrier and then sterilized linen or paper towels. The instruments will have been sterilized by heat in the autoclave already mentioned. For some complicated operations today, not this one on the appendix, different kinds of antiseptic chemicals are used to sterilize any special instrument which cannot be rendered bacteria-free by heat or atomic irradiation without damage to the instrument itself.

Right   Against sepsis—filtered air enters the operating theatre through openings in the ceiling and escapes near floor level through vents and louvres in the walls and doors.

The patient, now asleep and in an operation gown, accompanied by the anaesthetist, the nurse with the instruments, the surgeon and the assistant, meet at the operating table. Also the air meets the patient, coming into the theatre after it has been filtered. It is conducted into the theatre through vents in the ceiling, as a downdraught under positive pressure and it escapes through vents at floor level. Bacterial contamination in the theatre, including that caused by general activity and talking, can be monitored (tested) from time to time by putting down culture plates on the floor. Any bacteria which have fallen on them will grow in an incubator to form a little colony and can then be identified. The care taken in the way a theatre is ventilated is a reminder of the work of Pasteur and also of Lister's idea of using a carbolic spray (Chapter 7).

The patient's abdomen is now exposed and the surgeon is handed forceps into which are clipped small cotton swabs which have been dipped into an antiseptic solution (for example, iodine, alcohol, a mercury solution, chlorhexidine). The whole area where the incision is to be made and the skin around it are painted with this skin preparation ("skin prep"), two or three times. It has been found best to allow this antiseptic to dry on the skin. Sterile paper or linen towels are arranged to cover the body, leaving the operation site exposed. Sometimes small towels will be clipped to the wound during the operation and they may be called "percs"—a word which reminds us of the days when Lister and his followers always used towels soaked in, and therefore sterilized by, perchloride of mercury.

All is ready to begin the appendicectomy, but before the opening is made with the scalpel the surgeon may pause just for a second or two to check that everything is ready and to think about the particular task ahead. Lister would stand in silence with his head bowed. We also pause to consider how much

Top right Against sepsis— painting the skin with an antiseptic solution. The surgeon is pointing to the position of the appendix.

Bottom right Against sepsis— towels in place. The surgeon, now standing on the right of the patient, is about to make the incision with the scalpel, but in doing so breaks through the body's barrier to sepsis—the skin.

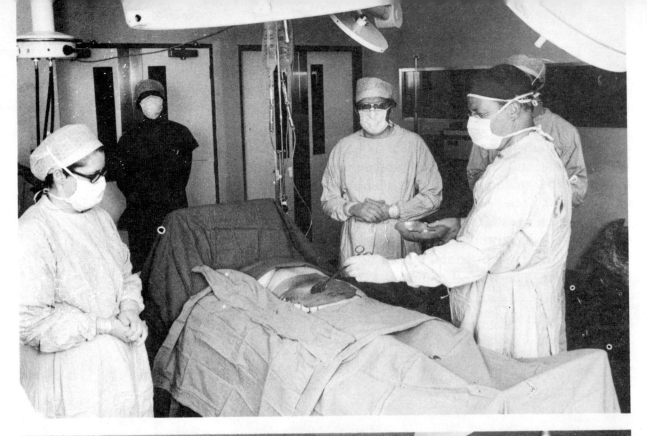
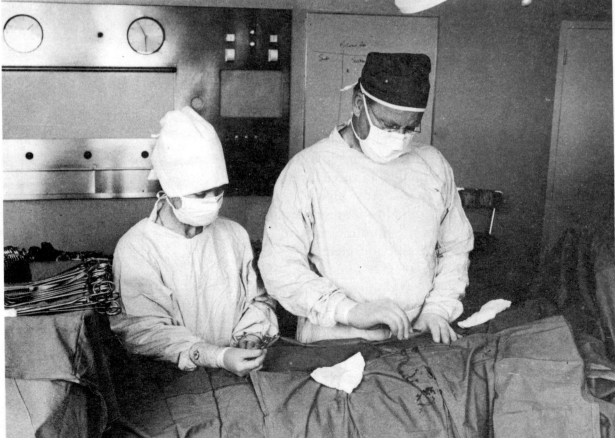

preparation has already gone into the operation before it has actually begun. Lister said that one of the greatest objections by others to his antiseptic system was that one had to take a lot of trouble over it. But we know that the trouble he took resulted in live patients. Still today one cannot perform operations without making antiseptic preparations, some of which have been described above.

The surgeon takes up the scalpel and presses the razor-sharp edge through, and draws it along, the skin in the line of the intended wound, over the site of the appendix. The wound might be 7·5–10 cm (3–4

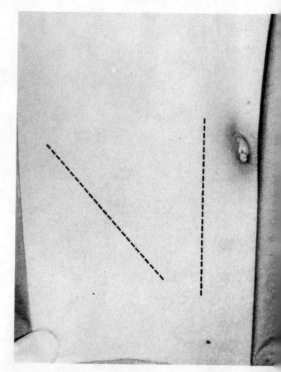

Top right   The dotted lines show two of the several possible incisions used for appendicectomy (appendectomy).

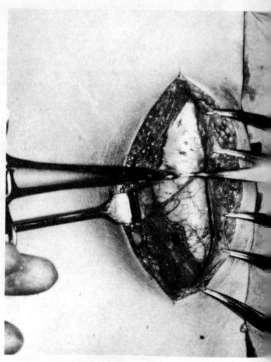

Bottom right   The surgeon has chosen the vertical incision. The muscular tissue is held aside (retracted) and the lining of the abdomen, the peritoneum, is held for the opening to be made into the peritoneal cavity.

inches) long, sometimes longer. Then he has to cut through the fat under the skin, and he separates or cuts the different muscles which lie in three layers to form the wall of the abdomen. Any blood vessel which has been cut across is caught in forceps and is tied by a ligature (Chapter 7). Sometimes a form of intense heat, generated by induction electricity on the points of special forceps is used to seal the vessels (diathermy). The cavity of the abdomen is lined with a sensitive membrane, the peritoneum, and this too has to be held up and then cut open with the scalpel. The coils of intestine are revealed. The surgeon

Top right The gangrenous appendix is held up with tissue forceps. The left-hand forceps indicate the attachment of the appendix to the caecum.

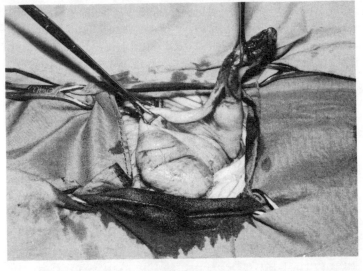

inserts his forefinger into the peritoneal cavity to find and deliver the red, inflamed appendix into the wound, or perhaps the caecum is found and rotated to expose the appendix.

Sterile packs made of cotton gauze are used to isolate the appendix from the edges of the wound to reduce the chance of bacterial contamination. Many surgeons still prefer that these be first wrung out in an antiseptic chemical. The surgeon now uses forceps to compress the artery to the appendix so that it can be

Bottom right Against sepsis—this picture portrays the value of Lister's work on sterilized catgut (see Chapter 7, Surgical Materials). The artery to the appendix has been clamped and then tied with catgut. The clamp is being removed. The catgut ends are cut by the scissors so that the ligatured artery can safely fall back inside the patient. This was not possible before Lister.

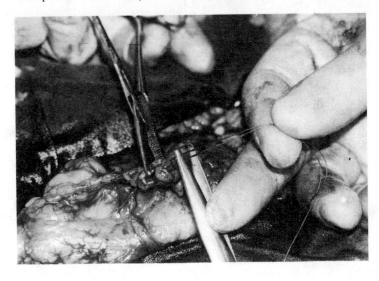

cut and tied with a ligature probably made from silk. The base of the appendix is then crushed and ligatured with catgut or silk (Chapter 7) so that the acutely inflamed appendix can now be cut out.

Often the stump of the appendix is buried by bringing the walls of the caecum together over it, using catgut threaded on a small curved needle. One more look is needed to make sure that there is no bleeding. The caecum is carefully returned into the abdominal cavity. All gauze swabs are removed, the surgeon changes his gloves, and one by one the layers of the abdominal wall are sewn together with catgut. The instrument nurse will announce in a clear voice that she has accounted for all the swabs and instruments that have been used. The skin wound in this particular case is likely to be sewn up with silk stitches.

The wound is then treated, perhaps even sprayed, with an antiseptic which is allowed to dry. A dressing is applied. This dressing has, of course, been sterilized, though not with an antiseptic. It is nevertheless an antiseptic barrier to contamination and is the modern equivalent of Lister's original dressing. All the towels are removed and by this time the patient is beginning to wake up.

What happens now within the wound will be exactly as described so beautifully by Lister (Chapter 5) when he studied inflammation. Also some cells from the body will mop up any dead particles, or stray bacteria. Other cells will provide the chemical darning material (collagen). A small scab will seal off the wound, and this will fall off as the skin cells join up together to form the natural barrier against sepsis. This is called healing by first intention—what we intend the wound to do if possible.

But supposing the appendix was very gangrenous and the bacteria very powerful (virulent). It might happen that the inflammatory reaction was more severe, resulting in an abscess of the wound. Possibly

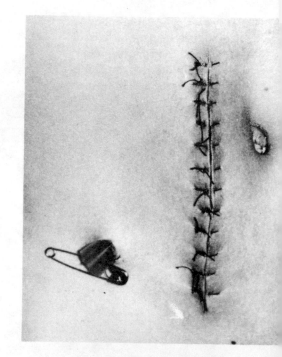

LISTER C
CONF
April 2nd

Patron: H

In March and April, 1867, Lo
technique were published and
this Centenary a Conference
Surgeons of England from 2nd

The theme of

SAFE

**The understanding and av
associated wi**

The Lister Oration 'Surgery and Liste
of Wimbledon (Lister Medalli

88

Top left The internal wound has been sewn together with catgut, and silk has been used to unite the skin. A popular method of stitching used here (vertical mattress sutures) probably came to King's College Hospital from Edinburgh via Lister. A small piece of rubber drain, shown here, may be used to drain the wound of any blood and serum and reduce the chances of sepsis. Lister also fixed his rubber tube with a safety pin. It stops the drain disappearing inside the patient.

Below The theme of the 1967 Lister Centenary Conference was "Safe Surgery". Lister will always be acknowledged as the man who made surgery safe.

NTENARY

ENCE

h, 1967

e Queen

's first reports on the antiseptic
nted to the world. To celebrate
held at the Royal College of
ril, 1967.

rence will be :

RGERY

of morbidity and mortality
on and injury

given by the Rt. Hon. the Lord Brock
t 4 p.m. on Tuesday, 4th April

this might have to be opened up by taking out a stitch in the skin and using the same kind of forceps that Lister used on Queen Victoria. Even a drainage tube might be needed (Chapter 7). The wound would not heal by first intention and it would be necessary for dressings to be applied every day. Carbolic acid would not be used, but sterilized dressings and some other kind of antiseptic chemical. Frequently we use a solution containing chlorine, a solution which had its origins in Edinburgh University and is, therefore, called EUSOL (Edinburgh University SOLution). Eventually the wound will fill up and the skin will close over. This is called healing by second intention.

Throughout this description of the preparation for and performance of this common operation it should have been easy to follow the influence of Lister and his work. Today, many surgeons may have forgotten that Lister is the source of so much that goes into making an operation safe. But they never forget the principle that at every step of an operation they are anti sepsis (against sepsis). If they are not anti sepsis, or if they forget the principle, their patients' lives may well be in unnecessary peril. As Lister said:

"With this as your guiding principle, you will find yourselves successful with the antiseptic system of treatment; but without it, whatever theory you adopt, you will ever be walking in the dark, and, therefore, ever liable to stumble."

It is right to remember that the great surgeons of today or tomorrow can only reach out to perform new and improved operations by standing on the shoulders of the giants of the past. Lister is one of these giants, a gentle, serious giant, whose sword against disease was his microscope, his shield was his research, his breastplate came from his lifelong interest in nature study, and his courage stemmed from his Christian outlook and upbringing.

Date Chart

1827	Joseph Lister born on the 5th April, at Upton House, West Ham, London.
1835	Writes to King William IV.
1835–44	Goes to Quaker schools at Hitchin and Tottenham.
1844–47	Studies for matriculation and Bachelor of Arts Degree of University of London at University College.
1848	Has smallpox and a nervous breakdown. Becomes a medical student at University College Hospital.
1850	Qualifies as a doctor. Wins University Gold Medals.
1851	Takes his microscope on holiday to Shanklin. Is house surgeon and house physician at University College Hospital.
1852	Becomes a Fellow of the Royal College of Surgeons of England (FRCS).
1853	His first two papers are published, on the eye and skin, based on research carried out as a student.
1853–55	Takes lodgings in Edinburgh. Works under Professor Syme. Falls in love with surgery and the Professor's daughter, Agnes. Becomes a Fellow of the Royal College of Surgeons of Edinburgh. Begins lectures and his research on inflammation.
1856	Resigns from the Quakers to marry Agnes Syme. Assistant Surgeon to the Royal Infirmary, Edinburgh.
1860	Appointed Regius Professor of Surgery at Glasgow. Elected Fellow of the Royal Society (FRS).
1861	Allowed the use of beds at the Royal Infirmary, Glasgow. Plans new operations and new instruments. Advances in surgery are paralysed by sepsis.
1865	Learns about the germ theory of Louis Pasteur, and the use of carbolic acid as a disinfectant of sewage. Uses a crude carbolic (German creosote) in dressings of wounds. Failure and success.
1867	Publication in *The Lancet* of his new treatment of compound fractures and abscesses based on the use of carbolic acid. Successfully prevents hospital sepsis. New horizons in surgery are opened up. Applies the antiseptic principle to the preparation of germ-free ligatures and surgical materials.

1869	Appointed Professor in Edinburgh. Develops the carbolic acid spray (abandoned 1887). Lister's father dies. Professor Saxtorph comes from Denmark.
1871	Operates on Queen Victoria. Improvises the rubber drainage tube. Researches into the bacteriology of milk. Draws the *Penicillium* mould.
1875	Correspondence with Queen Victoria about vivisection. Professor Nussbaum of Germany pays Lister a great tribute.
1876	Appointed to General Medical Council. Spreads his doctrine in Philadelphia, USA.
1877	Moves to London as Professor of Surgery at King's College Hospital. Mends a fractured patella with wire.
1879	Final acceptance of the antiseptic system. Remarkable scenes of acclamation in Amsterdam.
1880	Member of Council (later Vice President) of the Royal College of Surgeons of England.
1883	Baronetcy conferred—Sir Joseph Lister.
1891	British Institute of Preventive Medicine established (named the Lister Institute in 1903).
1892	Historic meeting with Pasteur in Paris.
1893	Sir Joseph Lister retires. Lady Lister dies in Italy.
1895	Elected President of the Royal Society.
1896	President of the British Association for the Advancement of Science.
1897	Becomes Lord Lister of Lyme Regis.
1902	Order of Merit. Privy Councillor.
1903	Eyesight begins to fail.
1909	Leaves London for Walmer, Kent.
1912	Lister dies at Walmer, Kent on 10th February. Service in Westminster Abbey. Buried in Hampstead Cemetery beside his wife.

Glossary

Abscess A collection of pus in the body.

Achromatic lens A lens which will transmit light without breaking the light into the colours of the rainbow.

Abdomen The belly, containing the abdominal organs such as the stomach, liver, intestines and kidneys.

Aorta The largest artery in the body, situated within the chest and abdomen.

Appendix Known as the vermiform appendix, meaning it is worm-like. The cul-de-sac extension of the part of the intestines known as the caecum.

Arteries The blood vessels conducting oxygenated blood under pressure from the heart to all the tissues of the body.

Antisepsis Literally, against sepsis.

Antiseptic Anything which stops decay.

Axilla The armpit.

Antiseptic principle Any measure taken to prevent or destroy bacteria causing sepsis.

Asepsis Without sepsis. Measures taken to exclude sepsis. Really part of antisepsis.

Bacteria Minute living forms (singular = bacterium) found in the soil, the dust and on the body. Also called germs, microbes, micro-organisms. Bacteriology is the study of bacteria.

Caecum The point at which the small intestine becomes the large intestine. The appendix is located here.

Camera lucida An instrument by which the image of an object is reflected through a glass prism on to paper so that its outline may be traced.

Capillaries The tiny blood vessels which conduct the blood amongst the cells of the body. Blood enters the capillaries by small arteries and leaves by the veins, to return to the heart.

Carbolic acid Also known as Phenol, found in coal tar.

Cell A living unit containing nucleus and protoplasm. Lister often referred to the living vitality of cells, a vitality which can ward off the attack of bacteria. He often said "living cells are the best antiseptic".

Cholera A severe illness affecting the intestines.

Coagulation Clotting of blood.

Corpuscles Red blood corpuscles carry oxygen to the cells. White corpuscles can envelop bacteria and act as scavengers.

Collagen The tough fibrous substance made by certain cells which binds the tissues together and is the repair material.

Corrosive sublimate Mercury perchloride. A poison to bacteria, and to humans if swallowed.

Cross infection The spread of infection from one person to another, particularly in hospital wards.

Fracture A broken bone. If there is any break in the skin it is called a compound fracture.

Germs Bacteria (see above).

Hypothesis An idea based on a reasoned argument to be proved or disproved by facts or experiments.

Infection Invasion of the body by bacteria, viruses, and fungi.

Inflammation The reaction of the living body to injury, infection by bacteria and infestation by parasites. Usually indicated by redness, pain, swelling, local heat and loss of function.

Ligature A piece of silk, thread, catgut or wire, or other material used to tie a blood vessel.

Microbes Bacteria (see above).

Microbiology The study of all minute living things—fungi, viruses and bacteria.

Pus The liquid contents of an abscess, containing live and dead bacteria, dead white blood corpuscles and other dead cells of the body.

Putrefaction Rotting or decaying of human or animal flesh.

Reduction In the case of fractured bones, it means putting the bone together as near as possible to its former state.

Scab The tough crust which is formed over a wound.

Sepsis Decay and poisoning arising from bacterial infection.

Septicaemia The presence of living and multiplying bacteria in the blood. Sepsis in the blood. Blood poisoning.

Sterilize To render something bacteria-free.

Suture Material used for stitching in operations (see ligature). To suture means to sew.

Further Reading

There are many books about the life and work of Lord Lister, and there are his own collected papers. The biography by Sir Rickman Godlee is the principal reference book because the author was Lister's nephew and assistant and so knew what went on in the great man's mind. Sir Rickman became President of the Royal College of Surgeons.

Lord Lister, Sir Rickman John Godlee Oxford: Clarendon Press 1924. 3rd edition.

Lister as I Knew Him, J R Leeson (Baillière, Tindall and Cox, 1927).

Lister and His Achievement, Sir William Watson Cheyne (Longmans Green, 1925).

Lord Lister, His Life and Work, G T Wrench (Fisher Unwin, 1913).

The Collected Papers, Baron Joseph Lister (Clarendon Press, Oxford, 1908).

British Journal of Surgery. Vol 54, Special Lister Number. (John Wright, Bristol, 1967).

Joseph Lister. The Man who Made Surgery Safe, F F Cartwright (Weidenfeld and Nicholson, 1963).

Lord Lister, His Life and Doctrine, D Guthrie (Livingstone, 1949).

Joseph Lister. Father of Modern Surgery, Rhoda Truax (Harrap, 1947).

Index

Picture Credits

The author and publishers wish to thank all those who have given their kind permission for illustrations to appear on the following pages: Johnson & Johnson, 55, 61; King's College Hospital Medical School, 45, 66/67, 71 (bottom), 72; Library of the Society of Friends, 12; Mansell Collection, 21, 24/25, 28/29, 33, 49, 74, 75, 77; Mary Evans Picture Library, 57 (bottom); Royal College of Surgeons of England, 19, 30, 35 (top), 36, 37, 39, 47, 50/51, 54 (left), 57 (top), 58/59, 60, 62, 65, 68, 78; Smith & Nephew Ltd, 8, 48, 54 (right), 56, 76, 79; University College Hospital Medical School, 13, 38, 71 (top); United States Information Service, 28; Wayland Picture Library, 22/23, 26, 34; Wellcome Institute for the History of Medicine, 20, 31, 32 (top), 41, 42, 43.

Illustrations on pages 2 (frontispiece), 16, 18 and 40 are reproduced from John Logan Turner's book *Lord Lister, 1827–1927*. Illustrations on pages 10, 11, 14, 15, 17, 32 (bottom), 35 (bottom), 52 and 63 and reproduced from Sir Rickman Godlee's book *Lord Lister,* for which the illustrations were prepared by Emery Walker.

Illustrations from the Wellcome Institute appear by courtesy of the Wellcome Trustees.

The publishers would like to extend especial thanks to the author, who organized the photographs on pages 81 to 89, and to the Medical Illustration Department of Charing Cross Hospital Medical School.

Richard Morris (Editor), August, 1977.